Making the Right Move:

Housing Options for Seniors

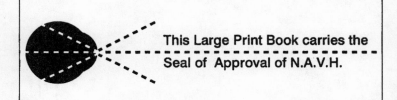

This Large Print Book carries the
Seal of Approval of N.A.V.H.

Making the Right Move:

Housing Options for Seniors

Gillian Eades Telford,

RN, BSN, LTCAC, MES

Thorndike Press • Waterville, Maine

Published in 2006 by arrangement with Self-Counsel Press.

Thorndike Press® Large Print Home, Health, and Learning.

The tree indicium is a trademark of Thorndike Press.

The text of this Large Print edition is unabridged.
Other aspects of the book may vary from the original edition.

Set in 16 pt. Plantin.

Printed in the United States on permanent paper.

Library of Congress Cataloging-in-Publication Data

Telford, Gillian Eades.
    Making the right move : housing options for seniors / by
Gillian Eades Telford. — Large print ed.
        p. cm.
    Originally published: Self-Counsel Press, 2004.
    ISBN 0-7862-8869-8 (lg. print : hc : alk. paper)
    1. Older people — Housing.   2. Nursing homes.
3. Older people — Care.   4. Large type books.   I. Title.
HD7287.9.T45 2006
    363.5′946—dc22   2006014926

This book is dedicated to my mother and her many friends.

Acknowledgments

At York University in Toronto, my thesis advisor, Dr. Trevor Hancock, reaffirmed my belief in health. He put into words what I had been feeling all my working life. He explained that what we have is not a health system, but a "sick care system." His article, *Mandala of Health: A Model of the Human Ecosystem*, pictured for me why I had always felt I was swimming against the stream when working for the health system. (Hancock, T. & Perkins, "Mandala of health: A model of the human ecosystem," *Family & Community Health*, 8(3), 1985: 1–10.) He affirmed that health encompasses so much more than hospital or community care. Meeting and then working with Dr. Hancock for two years was an epiphany for me. I had found someone else who felt as I did and who could so clearly verbalize the problems I had experienced.

I also want to thank Chris Somerville for encouraging me to write this book. Anne Woodson was a true inspiration and helped me by telling stories and writing and analyzing the questions in the questionnaires, using her considerable expertise as a clinical nurse specialist. Other people who helped and encouraged me include Dr. John Gray, Laura Koch, Barbra Armstrong, Dick Towson, Mark Dwor, Katherine Cobb, my daughter Barbara Telford, and my brother Robert Eades. A special thank you goes to my American law advisor, Greg Thulin, and Dr. Ruth Craven at the University of Washington School of Nursing.

This book could never have been completed without the help of the more than 20 directors of care who took the time out of their busy schedules to answer my questions and give me a tour through their facilities. The book would never have been finished without the editing help of Lynne Henderson.

Contents

Introduction

MAKING AN INFORMED CHOICE

Today's elders are more concerned than ever about the quality of care in nursing homes. Health Canada studies show that more than 80 percent of elders consider the availability of chronic, extended care, or nursing home beds for those who need them to be "very important." Unfortunately, many people are forced to make the decision to move to a nursing home when they are in a crisis or are sick and cannot bear to cope any longer in their present setting. At times like these, moving becomes imperative, and a decision made quickly may be uninformed.

About This Book
Making the Right Move is designed to help you make good, informed choices about your health and the places where you will live. It will encourage and empower you to consider your options before you are in a crisis so that you are aware of all the fac-

15

tors that can affect this important decision.

Choosing a nursing home for yourself or a loved one is a major life decision. After all, you have decided to move after a lifetime of independent living where you have managed to cope on your own — often with increasing physical and mental chronic conditions. You now realize that you need some help with your day-to-day activities.

But having to leave your family home does not mean that you have not successfully aged. All it means is that you now need a little help. Part One of this book discusses how to cope with the physical, mental, and spiritual aspects of aging. It then explains how the health care system works in the United States and Canada and helps you determine what level of care you may need. Part One also introduces you to the many housing options that are available to elders, from congregate living to 24-hour specialized nursing care. Remember, a nursing home is only one example of supportive housing available to you.

Part Two is designed to help you choose a facility that will provide you with quality care suitable to your needs. Using questionnaires that allow you to assess and compare facilities, this section of the book examines the components of quality care and considers what to do when you feel you are not receiving the appropriate level of care.

As you visit potential facilities and work through the questionnaires, keep in mind that the place you choose will be your new home — and it should feel that way. You should feel comfortable both with the level of care you are receiving and with your surroundings. Choosing a new home can be stressful. You may feel pressures from your children, your friends, even the staff of the facilities you are visiting. Take your time and choose the solution that is best for you.

Who This Book Is For

Making the Right Move is written for the elder who is considering his or her own future care. However, in many cases, children, spouses, or other relatives either assist in making this choice or are forced to make an independent decision themselves, usually because of a crisis. This book will provide assistance and guidance to both families and elders, giving them specific questions to probe their health care system and helping them to make the best choice to everyone's satisfaction.

Many elders who have partners are concerned about what will happen when one of them requires additional care. Although most nursing homes have accommodation for at least one couple, usually each elder in the couple has very different needs. For example, one spouse may need special nursing care at odd times of the day and night, and that may disturb his or her roommate. Unfortunately, nursing homes are not very adaptable to this kind of situation in their physical environment or in providing the different levels of care, although they are improving.

More and more multilevel homes are being built that allow couples to be housed in the same complex, if not in the same room or building. The most frequent scenario for couples is that one spouse will enter a nursing home while the other visits daily for long periods. The visiting spouse, or caregiver, still plays an important role as he or she does the extra little things that make life more comfortable for his or her spouse. One of the downsides to this arrangement, however, is that when couples are living as a pair, their pension may be adequate. But when separated, the pension does not cover two places of accommodation. This problem can motivate couples into incredible coping arrangements.

By 2010, 60 percent of people over age 50 will have a surviving parent, compared with only 16 percent in 1960. One of the fears of many elders is that their children will abandon them forever, placing them in a nursing home to die alone and uncared for. This fear along with failing health can make some elders cantankerous. They use all their resources, mental whiles, and emotional blackmail to try to persuade their families that they can live independently.

This emotional turmoil and underlying fear translates into guilt for their families. The process of deciding to place a family member in a nursing home is not easy, especially for the chief caregiver. The caregivers may feel a sense of failure and guilt that they cannot cope any longer. They may also experience a sense of loss because, in many cases, caring for that person has given their lives purpose and meaning. This is especially true of spouses. Many spouses will exhaust themselves to the point of illness rather than enlist formal help.

While families generally share the care of their beloved elders, the majority of the care giving usually falls on one person, most often the daughter or the daughter-in-law. The chief caregiver is the one who will bear the brunt of the emotional warfare that goes on before the decision is made to change housing arrangements.

To ease that tension, try to find out what the elder in your life wants in terms of living arrangements. If his or her expectations are not practical or realistic, then you may need to explain as gently as possible how difficult it is to spend quality time with him or her when you are also having to act as caregiver. Health care professionals advocate the concept of aging in place (see later in this chapter), but it is not possible if the family cannot accommodate the elder. The best plans work when an elder makes a decision in concert with his or her family.

By using this book as a reference to ensure you have made the best choice, you can help allay some of the guilt and frustration of placing someone you love in a nursing home, knowing you have done your best in their best interests.

Underlying Principles

This book is the result of my 25 years of practical experience in the field of elder care. As a gerontologist and previous director of care of a nursing home, I have worked with countless people to help them choose nursing homes and other supportive housing for themselves, their spouses, or their parents.

I have based my discussion on four major premises that are interwoven throughout the book, each of which is described in the following sections.

Language

The first premise is that language used to name people denotes values. The term "elders" refers to people over the age of 65, although the majority of elders in nursing homes are over the age of 85. I have used this term because it denotes an aura of respect and wisdom. It is the term used by aboriginal people for older adults, who are revered in their communities.

It is imperative that we show respect for elders. Infirmity and frailty are not reasons to treat people any differently from anyone else. Respect can be shown by the way people address each other, by the choices clients are given as well as in the general planning of all activities and the set-up of the environment.

Another term frequently used in the book is "client." I have used this term instead of "consumer," "patient," "resident," or "individual" because it connotes power. A client has the respect of service providers, and nursing homes provide a service of care as well as housing.

Aging in place

The second premise is that aging in place is a positive concept. When you age in place, you live in the same community (although not necessarily in the same residence) until you die. Most elders prefer to live and die at home, where they are surrounded by familiarity. In fact, 90 percent of today's elders live independently in their community (i.e., in an apartment, condominium, townhouse, duplex, or free-standing house). They are able to do most things for themselves, although some care is provided by family members or friends (informal help) or paid home care workers (formal help).

Other elders may choose to live in a nursing home or other facility such as Abbeyfield housing or congregate care. If that facility is in a community with which they are familiar, they will also be aging in place.

Definition of health

The third premise is that a broad definition of health is being used. According to the World Health Organization, "health is the extent to which an individual or group is able, on one hand, to realize aspirations and safety needs; and on the other hand, to change or cope with the environment. Health is therefore seen as a resource for everyday living, not the object of living; it is a positive concept emphasizing social and personal resources as well as physical capacity." In other words, health is influenced by many factors, including where you live, how you eat, how you exercise, and how many friends you have.

Client centeredness

The fourth premise is that any service organization should put the client first. Nursing homes are in the business of providing a caring service. Therefore the client must come first. For example, a nursing home that has set visiting hours is not client centered. Set visiting hours enable staff to do their work unencumbered by visitors. But people living at home don't generally have visiting hours for guests. A client-centered nursing home would allow clients to receive visitors whenever it suits them.

Chapter 6 discusses the concept of client centeredness in more detail.

Conclusion

Most of the definitions in *Making the Right Move* are from literature published by British Columbia's Ministry of Health and Ministry Responsible for Seniors. However, the general concepts of elder health care may be applied wherever you live in North America or around the world.

Throughout the book, I have used personal stories to illustrate how the complicated health care system works. All the stories are true, although the names have been changed for reasons of privacy.

The elders of today are mothers and fathers of the leading-edge baby boomers who are now in their 50s. At each stage of their lives, boomers have changed systems and institutions such as schools and universities. So too will they change the health system and the use of nursing homes. Already health care cuts have resulted in longer line-ups for surgery and limits in home care. This makes it all the more important for you to consider your options so that you can make the right move on terms that suit you.

Case Study

A Nursing Home Success: Mr. McKenzie's Story

Mr. McKenzie lived alone since his wife died. His children lived across the country, and while they phoned occasionally, he had lost interest in their lives and was depressed about his own life. Although Mr. McKenzie had been an active volunteer for the Lions Club, over the years, he had lost interest in anything to do with his community. At 87 years old, he just did not feel well enough, and it was too much effort to go out. He just sat in a chair all day watching TV.

His diabetes was out of control because he wasn't eating properly, and he had a huge ulcer on his right ankle that refused to heal. Diabetes and lack of circulation were not his only problems. He had congestive heart failure that made him short of breath even when he was moving slowly between his living room and kitchen. Arthritis made his joints hurt all the time, especially his hips and knees.

When Mr. McKenzie's daughter came out

for a visit one summer, she was shocked to see his horrid condition. She took him to his doctor, who suggested that he should consider moving into a nursing home because he needed care. Although he was not happy at the prospect, his daughter convinced him that it was the best solution.

Having made the decision, Mr. McKenzie and his daughter talked with a couple of different nursing home operators, before choosing Golden Years Nursing Home as his new home. Although Golden Years was across town from his grandchildren, whom he liked to visit, it was close to downtown, where the action was. The home also had a private room available, which was an essential requirement for Mr. McKenzie, who could not contemplate having a roommate after living alone all these years.

Now, after only three short months of living at Golden Years, Mr. McKenzie is a different person. His medical conditions have all improved dramatically. He eats well and now only needs a small pill for his diabetes. His congestive heart failure is under control through medication, and the ulcer on his leg has cleared up with the use of a new medicated dressing. Even his arthritis is not such a problem because he is doing weights three times a week in the gym under the direction of the physiotherapist.

He is also much happier than when he lived on his own. He is well-groomed, with his beard neatly trimmed. His clothes are pressed and clean, and his shoes are shiny. He is an early riser, so he has breakfast from the hot steam table set near the kitchen for all early risers like him. They have a breakfast group of about eight people. The other clients cherish Mr. McKenzie because he is one of the few men in the home. The women and the staff really like him. He even has a new girlfriend, Pam, who comes to see him daily. He is busy. He loves woodworking in the shop and making toys for his great grandchildren. Pub nights are his favorite night of the week when Pam joins him. Because of her, he even goes to church again, and they meet yet another time in the week on this outing.

The computer club is a boon to his existence. He is now in touch with his kids and plays bridge on the Internet because he is above the level of the players in this home. He gets on a chat-line early in the morning with his daughter who is in a different time zone. Mr. McKenzie has a new outlook on life. It is fun again. He looks forward to new developments each day.

Learning the computer was a long process for him. The activity director at Golden Years spent many hours patiently teaching him, and fortunately, all that time has paid off: he now teaches other elders and leads the computer group that meets three times a week.

In fact, Mr. McKenzie is feeling and doing so well that he is thinking of moving into the independent-living apartment complex next door. He could still see all his new friends, participate in the activities as he chooses, and have all his meals provided. In addition, he is thinking he could marry Pam so they can do these activities together.

Mr. McKenzie's success story shows how admission to a nursing home can be a positive experience. The nursing homes of today are not all filled with sick, crazy people who don't know where they are, nor do the facilities have an aura of gloom, darkness, and hopelessness. They can be very attractive, positive places to live, and many people thrive and improve wonderfully after admission because they receive the care they need and are no longer lonely, isolated, or bored.

PART ONE

Choosing the Care That Is Right for You

Chapter 1

AGING SUCCESSFULLY

The following story illustrates the effect of a positive mind on a positive life. By maintaining balance in all areas of her life, Mrs. Stein manages to exemplify successful aging. In fact, gerontologists ought to be studying people like her to examine how she was able to survive so well.

Case Study
Aging Successfully: Mrs. Stein's Story

The sun shone on Mrs. Stein, making her silver hair sparkle as she sat on a bench under a tree outside her apartment. Her son had arranged a party for her 90th birthday, and the garden was filled with chatting groups of people, from high school girls, young married couples, and middle-aged matrons to dowagers and people her own age, all somehow connected to Mrs. Stein through her many varied activities.

Mrs. Stein was holding court, vivaciously telling stories. She introduced the man sitting next to her as her "latest squeeze," telling the story of how they had met and fallen in love. "He came to one of my lectures on Emily Brontë, and I went to one of his lectures about astronomy, and that was that." She had been divorced 35 years previously and had had no man in her life until now. She was an intellectual and a scholar on Emily Brontë and now she lectured at the senior's university alumni center.

Although Mrs. Stein had physical problems, she made light of them. She had arthritis in her knees, which made walking difficult. She had trouble seeing and needed very strong light and a strong magnifying glass to read. It was slow going, but she persisted and talked to her friends about what she had read. She even did needlepoint under the same circumstances, although the stitching was no longer as minuscule as it had been in her earlier work. Also, Mrs. Stein was getting deaf and had trouble hearing her classical music unless she turned it up quite high. By so doing, the deafness did not bother her. She could still hear people talking to her as long as background noise was minimal.

Mrs. Stein had always been active in the

affairs of her cooperative housing project and was responsible for drawing up the bylaws that governed their living. Her apartment co-op was an early government project with rent geared to income, so this helped to keep her financially independent and enabled her to pursue her many interests.

Mrs. Stein was known to the continuing care division of her regional health board and had a homemaker once a month to clean her apartment. She cooked for herself, and a neighbor got her groceries because she had stopped driving a couple of years ago.

Her only son lived out of town but came to visit every couple of months. She phoned him occasionally to keep in touch. Her family included her vast number of friends in the apartment townhouse complex, and she was always meeting new people and making new friends. She had a vast knowledge about many subjects, was terribly opinionated, but had a rare sense of humor and a delight in living that enchanted everyone.

She was interested and contributed to her community. She was responsible for establishing a group in a senior center that advocated for elder rights. Over the years, when she took an interest in anything, she devoted her great mind to seek solutions and solve problems. She was an activist, and some of her early efforts had flourished into growing organizations in which she was still involved in their daily affairs.

Making the Choice to Age Successfully

Aging is a beautiful, normal process. Aging successfully means living a long and healthy life. It is a personal task steeped in choices. How you act and how you think can to a large degree determine how well you age. By optimizing your strengths and compensating for your disabilities, you can overcome the challenges life throws at you.

Everyone has the capacity for change, no matter what age they may be. You are not in a process of inevitable decline, and you can be as active as you choose to be. Modern aging studies show that old ideas about aging are largely inaccurate. For example, it is not normal to be stiff and have trouble walking. Inactivity or illness causes this. Studies show that two-thirds of the signs usually attributed to aging are the result of disuse or disease, while only one-third is actually due to aging itself. In fact, normal aging does not result in slower, less efficient physical, mental, or spiritual activity.

Our motivations and actions are largely influenced by three factors: the body, mind, and spirit. The balance between these three can be delicate. Like Mrs. Stein, you may be vulnerable to physical, psychological, economic, social, and environmental challenges. For example, the pain and discomfort of disease may result in depression. Retiring from work may leave you with very little disposable income. Physical inactivity may prevent you from pursuing a social life, making you dependent on people coming to see you. This can lead to isolation and loneliness. You may be at risk of falling because of environmental hazards and adverse drug combinations. By consciously trying to balance your body, mind, and spirit, you can to a large degree reduce the effect of these challenges.

Dealing with the Physical Effects of Aging

Elders of today are surviving longer and living better than in the past. On the whole, they are a healthier group than they were a decade ago. In fact, as your children age, they will probably be healthier than you are. One of the major reasons that elders are living better is because less disability is caused by illness than in the past, and drugs control many symptoms.

Modern medicine has made great advances in curing acute illnesses. The discovery of antibiotics was a milestone in the cure of many acute illnesses such as ear infections, gall bladder infections, measles, mumps, rubella, and whooping cough. Advances in surgical techniques for replacement and removal of diseased body parts have contributed to fewer people dying from acute disease.

However, we are currently only managing, not curing, chronic illnesses such as arthritis (inflammation of the joints), osteoporosis (porous or holey bones that break easily), and macrimal deterioration (nerve-ending damage to the eye that leads to blindness). We can treat the symptoms, but not eliminate the cause.

Depending on the cause of your illness, medical, alternative, or nonmedical interventions may help increase your physical capacity. You may suffer from a chronic illness that affects your body, but in the process of coping, you may gain a new emotional sense of well-being in your mind.

Your body structure will change throughout your life. The changes start from the moment you are born. Take the skin, for example. A baby's skin is soft and flexible. The skin cells slough off as growth occurs until, in old age, the skin loses some of its elasticity and ability to be soft and flexible, which results in wrinkles and lines. The skin changes at different rates. Some 80-year-olds look no older than 60, and some 60-year-olds look older because of their wrinkled skin.

Your muscles also change as you develop from babyhood. However, if you continue to use your muscles, you will find that your physical capacity can be amazing. You may not have to change the way you live your life, as your body changes gradually and enables you to accommodate. So when you see elders doing physical activities such as hiking and skiing, you'll notice that they have more efficiency of movement and don't "hot rod" it up or down the hill as they did in their youth.

Physical well-being is a major part of happiness and life satisfaction. It provides you with the means to do what you want to do, when you want to do it, and it helps you achieve purpose in your life.

How to enhance your physical well-being

You may choose to enhance your physical body development through exercise. Consider some of the following tips for further taking care of your body:

* *Be aware of and strive for balance in your life between exercise, nutrition, and rest and relaxation.* Be cautious of the drugs you take, including non-prescription over-the-counter drugs, such as vitamins, allergy pills, herbal medicines, or laxatives. Know what medications you are taking and why. Medication can save your life, but too many drugs may react adversely and make you sick. Ask your physician or pharmacist about your medication.

* *Be energetic.* Don't slow down. Universal law dictates that natural order is ordained by only one mechanism: a well-directed, positive flow of energy. Endeavor to maintain your energy flow. You do not need to be slower as you get older.

* *Be in the habit of eating what nature first laid on your table.* Eat a generous

portion of fruits, vegetables, and lean meat. Your meals may be smaller and more often than in previous decades, but you still need good food to retain your energy. Indulge yourself by eating and drinking sensibly. Make the effort and take the time to prepare nourishing meals.

* *Be open to new learning.* Achieving a healthy body requires development and application of skills in such areas as self-awareness and lifestyle management.

* *Be persistent.* If the physician you consult dismisses your symptoms as a consequence of your age, seek a second opinion.

* *Be physically active.* Do at least 30 minutes of sustained rhythmic vigorous exercises four times a week. Seek out patterns, times, places, and contacts that make exercise as much a part of your life as eating and sleeping are. This may mean walking to a shopping area or joining the walking group in the mall.

* *Be rested.* Get as much sleep and rest as you need. Make quiet times a priority. Your sleep pattern may change

as you age. If you nap during the day, you may not sleep as long at night. But you need the overall hours of accumulated sleep.

* *Be sensitive to changes in your body and abrupt changes in your ability to function.* For example, if you notice changes such as difficulty in dressing or a loss of appetite, you should see a physician and get a thorough diagnostic exam.

Dealing with the Mental Effects of Aging

Although society is preoccupied with the effects of aging on bodies, gerontologists are discovering that a healthy mind and spirit are most important to successful aging. According to US statistics, 80 percent of elders in nursing homes have a significant mental health problem, with depression as the most common condition.

Your mind is your intellect and gives you the ability to learn, grow, and handle challenges. It provides you with the means to develop a purpose in life and to be happy. Having a healthy mind means you have the ability to establish and maintain intimacy with others and to tolerate and appreciate differences.

How to enhance your mental well-being

* *Be a risk-taker.* Life does not get better until you are willing to challenge yourself and do things that may be difficult. Accept the challenge. Take a trip.

* *Be a student.* Learn something new, such as computer skills. Your brain is as good as it ever was. Use it and rejoice in the knowledge that the ability to learn never dies. You live in an information age where there is ready access to infinitely new subjects.

* *Be an opportunist.* See difficulties as challenges that give you the opportunity to overcome them and experience success. Attend a lecture at the wellness center.

* *Be aware of the Golden Rule:* Do unto others as you would have them do unto you.

* *Be confrontational.* Be willing to confront people with issues that are important to you. Take responsibility for your part in the issue. Stand up for what you believe, and have your questions answered so you understand. Find a mutually satisfying solution.

* *Be open in your communication with others.* Tell people how you feel, and own your own feelings without blaming those feelings for your reactions. Listen to your grandchildren; within youth are many truths.

* *Be open-minded.* Be willing to hear another person's point of view without judgment. It doesn't have to agree with your own. Be willing to consider other possible facts, solutions to problems, and explanations.

* *Expand the perimeters of your awareness.* Accept that your children lead their own lives, and take an interest in what they are thinking. It's a fast-changing world.

* *Be positive about yourself.* Surround yourself with family and friends who validate you. You need encouragement and positive feedback as well as honest concern.

* *Be responsible for your life.* Your actions create consequences. Find solutions without blaming others. Maybe you are lonely. Have a conversation with the person who delivers your mail. See people every day and talk to them. Join a temple or a church.

Dealing with the Spiritual Effects of Aging

The basic concepts of spiritual health emphasize love, joy, peace, sense of purpose, and achieving your full potential. Having spiritual health does not necessarily mean you are religious. You may be spiritual but not identify with any religious group. Religion is a support resource for many elders because it provides hope and meaning to many.

Values formed over time are an extension of your attitude to life. Spiritual health is a process that reflects the intangible aspects of your quality of life. It involves taking a personal inner journey that is different for every person. Discovering or creating life meaning can raise you above pain and loss. In the pursuit of successful aging, spirituality is relevant and compelling.

How to enhance your spiritual well-being

* *Be a finisher.* Nature operates in such a way that growing and living are nearly synonymous. When one stops, so does the other. Complete that book or tapestry you have been working on for so long.

* *Be a goal-setter.* Set goals and accept

challenges that force you to be active.

* *Be creative.* Creativity is not confined to the first part of your life. In fact, accumulated knowledge and experience make the later decades more congenial to new accomplishments. Join an art group or a woodworking or calligraphy class.

* *Be happy.* Maintain your sense of humor. Make each day an opportunity for optimism for yourself and others. A positive mind creates expectations that something good is about to happen and opens doors to new options for success. Learn a new joke every day.

* *Be independent.* Don't depend on others for your well-being. A well-developed sense of who you are is the crucial link to a long and meaningful existence. We all need to maintain dignity, autonomy, and independence in our daily lives. Find a place to live where you have access to shopping, the library, your place of worship, and other necessary amenities.

* *Be kind to yourself.* Make time in your day to meditate, pray, or have quiet moments.

* *Be motivated, and see challenges as opportunities for change.* Difficulties in your life can be overcome if you regard them as opportunities. Do something to change your situation or emotional mindset. Join the senior's activity center near you.

* *Be necessary and responsible.* Live outside yourself. Volunteer your services. See each day as a chance to help someone or something. Associate with other active, involved individuals. Sharpen your sense of duty to preserve your environment, the earth that nurtures everyone. Do some gardening today.

* *Be positive.* Be willing to see different sides to a situation, and pursue a course of action and thinking that allows for positive changes, or acceptance of what is. Invite that old friend over for tea and mend the rift between you.

It is essential that you maintain balance in your life. Be aware that to be healthy, you need to pay attention to all parts of yourself. Successful aging means your body, mind, and spirit are used to capacity.

Chapter 2

THE HEALTH CARE SYSTEM

The health care system in North America is a complicated array of systems and services, and for many people, it is shrouded in mystery. This chapter follows the story of Mrs. Martino, whose encounters with the health system are quite typical for many elders. Research shows that family help is usually the first line of defense, and formal care provided by the health system is accepted only as the last resort. This chapter helps you understand the kinds of services available to elders and their families — before a crisis forces you to make a quick decision.

The health care systems in the United States and Canada are very different, so not all of the information in this chapter may apply to you. However, the basic concepts of the care needed for elders are the same wherever you live. Your doctor, regional health board, or local state department of social and health services can help you determine how to receive the best possible care for your needs.

The Health Care System in the United States

Because health care in the United States is not government subsidized, many people carry private health insurance (usually through their employers or unions). If you do not have private health insurance and you have no assets, you are covered under Medicaid. Medicaid is a federally supported, state-operated public assistance program that pays for health services for people with low incomes, including elderly or disabled persons who qualify. Medicaid pays for long-term nursing facility care; some limited home health services and may pay for some assisted living services depending on the state. Medicaid pays for the care of half of the clients in US skilled nursing facilities.

Medicare is the largest insurer in the United States and insures more than 40 million people. It is a federal health insurance program for people —

✱ age 65 and older,

✱ of any age with permanent kidney failure, and

* under 65 with certain disabilities.

Medicare provides primarily skilled medical care and medical insurance under the following schemes:

* Medicare Part A is hospital insurance that helps pay for inpatient hospital care, limited skilled nursing care, hospice care, and some home health care. Most people get Medicare Part A automatically when they retire as part of their social security benefits.

* Medicare Part B is medical insurance that helps pay for doctor's services, outpatient hospital care, and some other medical services that Part A does not cover (like home health care). You must pay a monthly premium to receive benefits under Part B. The cost in 2003 was $58.70 per month.

Medicare Supplemental Insurance (often called Medigap) is private health insurance that pays Medicare deductibles and coinsurances and may cover services not covered by Medicare. Most Medigap plans will help pay for skilled nursing care, but only when that care is not covered by Medicare.

Health maintenance organizations (HMOs), pre-provider organizations, provider sponsored organizations, and private fee-for-service organizations all contribute to Medicare-managed care plans. A professional or group of professionals from any of these organizations paid by Medicare oversees and provides medical services for the people they insure, including hospital care, home care, and long-term care. Since Medicare is a co-payment plan and rates differ depending on the services, the people they insure need to partially pay for these services. Bear in mind though, that the physicians in these organizations are the gatekeepers. To save the organization money, they can control the number of tests ordered and the type of treatment recommended. (**Note:** Medicare is for people 65 and older.)

Social health maintenance organizations (S/HMO) provide the full range of Medicare benefits offered by standard HMOs, plus additional services. These may include care coordination, prescription drug benefits, chronic care benefits covering short-term nursing home care, a full range of home and community based services such as a homemaker, personal care services, adult day care, respite care, and medical transportation. Other services may include eyeglasses, hearing aids, and dental benefits. Membership offers other health benefits that are not provided through Medicare alone or most other health plans for elders. There are currently four S/HMOs participating in Medicare: Portland, Oregon; Long Beach, California; Brooklyn, New York; and Las Vegas, Nevada.

The Health Care System in Canada

In Canada, basic health care is universal and free. This means that in each province everyone is entitled to see a physician and to have access to hospital care at no cost to the individual. The Canada Health Act's principle of portability means that care should be the same in each province. However, the Health Act refers to acute care hospitals, illness, and disease treatment by physicians — nothing else. While some provinces have chosen to include other aspects of health, such as home care, it is not consistent across the country. Some provinces include home care as a universal right, and others do not include it. Another gray area is long-term care. Some provinces include nursing home facilities as universal, others are pay as you go, and still others pay for different levels of nursing homes depending on your income.

Because of cutbacks to the Canadian health care system, many people also carry private health insurance to supplement their provincial benefits.

Case Study

The Health Care System: Mrs. Martino's Story

Mrs. Martino had moved into an apartment in the same neighborhood as her family home a few years after her husband died. There were many reasons for the move. The location of the family home was wrong: it was too difficult to get help up the hill, and the grocery stores were miles away. In the winter, she was snowed in for days at a time and she felt isolated because she couldn't drive in the snow and ice. The bus system was infrequent, and the bus stopped a few blocks away. By moving into an apartment in the same neighborhood, Mrs. Martino aged in place within her community but not in her dwelling.

Mrs. Martino had two children. Like her, her son and his family lived in Victoria, British Columbia, while her daughter and her family lived in Edmonton, Alberta. Socially, Mrs. Martino had a wide circle of friends. She had many interests and kept her mind and body occupied. She was a member of the nearby seniors' center and joined in exercise classes, crafts, and other activities. She loved playing Scrabble and bridge and kept her mind active through a study group. She also swam every day.

She was fiercely independent although, like so many other elders, she had a combination of chronic medical problems that had developed over the years and had been diagnosed and treated by the family physician.

Family physician and pharmacist

Mrs. Martino was a diabetic with a thyroid problem and congestive heart failure. She was also losing her sight because of macrimal degeneration and glaucoma, and had some hearing loss that was caused by a decrease in the size of her hearing canals. Under her family physician's direction, she was able to control these chronic conditions through medication and diet. She bought her medication from a pharmacist who always carefully explained what each medication was for and how and when to take it. Fortunately, these conditions were not a bother to her. She had no disability and could do everything she wanted.

Mrs. Martino's medical conditions are common to many elders and can be controlled through visits to the family physician, with occasional visits to specialists to confirm the management and treatment of the chronic conditions. Most elders visit a pharmacist to obtain their medication.

Activities of daily living

In medical terms, at this point, Mrs. Martino managed well with the activities of daily living (ADL). This means that she was able to cope with the actions essential to maintaining independence, such as walking on flat surfaces and stairs, being able to sit and get out of a chair or in and out of bed, being able to dress and bathe herself, and being able to do her teeth and hair and eat her meals. Medical professionals evaluate an elder's ability to perform these activities, and then use the results to assess how much care the person needs. (See more about assessment in Chapter 3.)

However, Mrs. Martino did need some help to accomplish some instrumental activities of daily living (IADL). IADLs are defined as actions that help elders do the essentials to remain independent, including shopping for food, house cleaning, banking, gardening, driving, or being able to walk longer distances or take public transit. Her son helped with her income taxes and some banking and drove her to the grocery store on occasion. She also had a cleaning person who helped clean her apartment.

An encounter with the regional health services

For her 80th birthday, Mrs. Martino took a cruise to Alaska. Unfortunately, she fell, badly breaking her ankle. There was no doctor aboard, so the freighter diverted and deposited her in an acute care hospital at the nearest port, where they operated on her ankle. Within three weeks, she was able to return home. She was fortunate to have purchased medical insurance; otherwise, the bill could have been thousands of dollars.

She was in a wheelchair when she was discharged from hospital with her leg in a cast. Although the physiotherapist had taught her how to walk on flat surfaces and up and down stairs with crutches, she was still weak.

On her return home, Mrs. Martino contacted her family physician, who instructed her to call the local health unit so she could receive some in-home help. The intake nurse arranged for an assessment by the continuing care division of her regional health board. Most regional health boards have a continuing care division of some kind. It may also be called the long-term, extended, or chronic care division. This division usually provides a comprehensive range of community-based, supportive health care services to assist people whose ability to function independently is affected by long-term (i.e., more than three months) health-related problems.

Mrs. Martino explained that she was living alone and that she had a number of chronic illnesses, besides the fact she was in a wheelchair with a broken ankle. Because she could not currently do many of the activities of daily living without assistance, she needed immediate help or she was at risk of being hospitalized again. She was assessed and was assigned a case manager, who worked closely with her family physician. The case manager is usually a registered nurse who can coordinate health care services, teach family members how to care for their elders, plan further client care based on a health assessment, and communicate with physicians regarding medical progress. Mrs. Martino's case manager decided that she needed the following homecare support:

* A resident care aide/nurse aide/homemaker who would help her bathe, dress, make her bed, prepare her meals and buy the food, and clean the apartment.

* A physiotherapist to give her exercises to help her regain her muscle tone and provide therapy to regain mobility. The physiotherapist also showed her son how to assist with these exercises. (Note: Many states and provinces charge a fee for physiotherapy services. Check with your state/province medical plan to see if these services are covered.)

* A nutritionist to provide instructions on how to prepare meals that accommodated her diet restrictions (i.e., foods low in sugar for her diabetes and low in salt for her heart condition).

* An occupational therapist to suggest ways she could make bathing, cooking, and cleaning easier as she became more mobile. (Occupational therapists also assess your physical and mental limitations and home facilities. They will recom-

mend changes, assistive devices, or adaptations in the environment to increase your independence.)

In a few short weeks after arriving back in her apartment, Mrs. Martino was able to maneuver the wheelchair; then graduated to a walker, crutches, and finally a cane. Six weeks later, she was able to do everything for herself, and she resumed her activities and social lifestyle.

Supportive Health Care Services

Through the supportive health care services offered in her community, Mrs. Martino was able to recuperate with relatively little difficulty. Supportive health care services is a generic term that includes many programs, not all of which may be available in your area. Some services may be government sponsored and others may be private. Your family doctor, hospital, HMO, Eldercare Locator, local health board, or senior services organization will be able to help you determine what services are available and how to contact them. Also see the section "How to Get in Touch with Health Care Services" at the end of this chapter. Following are some of the services they may provide:

Case management services

Professionally trained staff are usually available to help clients connect with the appropriate services needed. Case managers assess, consult, teach, and link clients to the most appropriate care providers. Case management is a good idea on paper, but in fact, case managers often have up to 350 clients. Often, only clients who are in crisis are managed because there is just no time to do a good job for everyone. Case managers in HMOs may have less of a caseload.

In-home support homemaker services

This long-term program may also be called home support, home care, continuing care, or community care. To qualify, you must be assessed by a nurse, social worker, physiotherapist, or occupational therapist. Most in-home support programs use homemakers with special training or resident care aides or certified nurse aides to assist elders with personal care such as bathing, dressing, and grooming.

Home care is usually free if you do not have much income; otherwise, payment is on a sliding scale depending on income. The assessors from the long-term care program in the continuing care division of the health unit look at your last income tax return to determine how much you will be asked to pay. If you have adequate income, you will have to pay well for the services you receive. Many private agencies that are not contracted to the regional health board charge less to clients for homemaker services than government-supported agencies. In the United States, home care may be covered under Medicare Part B or another private insurance plan, but certain conditions apply.

In-home care provides care appropriate to your needs as decided by the case manager. You are assigned a worker for a specified number of hours a day or week. Because of health care cutbacks, this service is often rationed in many communities, and is typically designed to enhance and complement the support you receive from family and friends. You can often purchase more hours of service from the agency that supplies your worker.

The regional health boards usually contract with an agency to have them provide home care. The agency may be either for profit or nonprofit, and there is no guarantee that you will get the same person each time. Although these agencies bid for government contracts at the regional health board level, no specific standards of care exist. So the quality of staff may vary from poor to superior.

Residential care services

Residential care services range from private luxury retirement homes to skilled nursing facilities or chronic/extended care nursing homes. In the United States, all nursing homes are private and the government does not subsidize care, so you will pay as you go. Medicare can cover some certified skilled nursing facilities, and Medicaid will pay for these same facilities if a client qualifies. Some nonprofit and religious homes, as well as Medicare and Medicaid homes, are available. You should check with your local health authority or senior services for more information.

In most Canadian provinces, residential care services operate under the auspices of the continuing care division of your local health authority. They are usually government supported and accessible to all elders who pay only the accommodation cost of $23 to $36 per day. The health care component is free because health care in Canada is free. Depending on the province in which you live, the number of hours of care is usually restricted to approximately 1.5 hours of nursing care in a 24-hour period per client. The care is supervised by a registered nurse, but most personal care activities are performed by resident care aides.

See Chapters 4 and 5 for more detailed information on the kinds of homes available.

Shared supportive living services

Also known as family care homes, these are single-family residences that care for up to two long-term care clients. These residences provide a protective, supportive, family life environment within a family home and are an alternative to admission to a nursing home facility. The Canadian government through the health department pays the family for the care of these clients. See Chapter 4 for more information on this kind of care.

In the US, adult family homes are the equivalent of Canadian family care homes. Adult family homes are privately owned, licensed, and regulated by the State. Medicaid or private pay will pay for the care.

Adult day-care programs

Adult day-care programs give respite to family caregivers. These programs usually operate from Monday to Friday and supply a hot noon meal, recreational activities, and social interaction for elders with physical or mental impairments. A few day-care programs can accommodate an elder overnight if the family is in crisis.

Special support services

Your regional health board may also supply meals, senior centers, adult day-care programs, and palliative and respite care.

Meal programs such as Meals on Wheels, Congregate Meals, or Wheels to Meals are run by volunteers but usually have a paid staff overseer. In the Meals on Wheels or Wheels to Meals programs, the hot and nutritious meals are provided for people who cannot do their own cooking. The client can purchase frozen meals for weekends. The food is usually prepared in a facility or government-inspected catering establishment where meals are wrapped, and volunteers deliver them to homes. The cost of meals is on a sliding scale depending on the client's income. Congregate Meals is a program where clients gather to eat in a common place. The food is prepared off-site, and is brought and served by volunteers.

Many senior centers have preventive and supportive health programs for elders, such as friendly visiting, free transportation, help with shopping, and help with legal questions, bill paying, or other financial matters.

Palliative care provides support for people who are dying. Usually, the elder will get an increase in the number of hours of care in the home so he or she may die at home. Respite care is provided to the family to relieve them of their responsibilities for a while so that they can continue with some of their day-to-day activities. Family members can book their elder into an intermediate care facility if they are going on holiday. Respite can also take place in the home, and workers will be provided on a 24-hour basis to take care of the client at home while the family has a break. The continuing care division of the health department usually pays respite care.

In the US, it depends on what medical insurance or Medicaid to which the person qualifies. Often respite care is private pay.

Case Study

An Encounter with the
Quick-Response Program

One morning, at age 82, Mrs. Martino was going to feed her fish in the half-barrel when she slipped on the icy patio. She managed to crawl to the phone and call 911. The ambulance arrived and took her to the nearest hospital emergency that had a quick-response program.

To reduce the use of expensive acute-care hospital beds, some HMOs and regional health boards have introduced programs that supply home care to clients on a short-term basis. A social worker usually arranges through a contracted agency to provide homemakers on a short-term basis of one to five days. Depending on an individual's situation and whether or not the health board has previously assessed him or her, the service may be free or based on the person's income.

Mrs. Martino was assessed by a physician, who determined that the only care she needed was bed rest while the vertebrae she broke during her fall healed. The emergency ward social worker called her son and told him that his mother could be discharged home, and she would receive home care for 16 hours a day for three days.

Unfortunately, it took longer than three days for her broken vertebrae to heal, so Mrs. Martino and her son needed to look beyond the quick-response program for help. If she had had no family, and if no interim rehabilitative places existed in her community, the hospital would have admitted her for a few weeks until she was sufficiently mobile to look after herself with some home care. Keeping her in the acute care hospital would have been a waste of those resources, however, because she really had no need for 24-hour care from registered nurses.

Luckily, Mrs. Martino had the support of her family, and her son arranged for a homemaker to help her while she recovered.

Assistive devices

During her recovery, Mrs. Martino was in a lot of pain. Her physician changed the type of painkillers she was on and also suggested she use some assistive devices. An assistive (or adaptive) device is a piece of equipment that assists the user in the operation of self-care, work, or leisure activities. Eyeglasses can be considered an assistive device. If an assistive device is deemed medically necessary, some insurers will cover the cost. For example, Medicare will pay for some medical equipment as long as the equipment —

* can withstand repeated use,

* is primarily and customarily used to serve a medical purpose,

* is generally not useful to a person in the absence of an illness or injury, and

* is appropriate for use in the home (e.g., wheelchairs, hospital beds, walkers).

Mrs. Martino purchased a TENS (transcutaneous electro nerve stimulator) machine. This machine reduced the need for medication by using an electrical current to cut the nerve pathways for pain. With the pain under control, she could lie on her side for short periods and eat comfortably.

However, she could not raise her head to watch TV, nor could she hold a book. So, for entertainment, the library provided "talking books" that kept her occupied when visitors were not there.

As time passed, Mrs. Martino became troubled by her loss of sight. She could not play Scrabble anymore because she could not keep score. Her son bought her a large-tiled Scrabble board, but not being able to keep score or read the dictionary made playing too difficult. Her son also bought her a large TV, and she learned the remote control buttons by experimenting and just turned the volume up until she could hear. Bridge was becoming a problem, even with the large playing cards. Usually one of the four could see well enough to score, but even using the big cards was getting difficult.

Transportation

She was still driving her car but not during the evening, because she knew she could not see at night. She did not want to give up driving because it gave her so much independence. Actually, Mrs. Martino was a menace on the road. Many jurisdictions require people over the age of 65 or those with a medical condition to take a driver's re-examination every couple of years. If you have trouble checking over your shoulder, or seeing at night or in poor weather, you may be putting yourself and others at risk.

It was past time for her to give up driving, but she had to make the decision herself. After an incident where she ended up driving on the sidewalk, she reluctantly stopped. It was one of the more difficult decisions for Mrs. Martino to make, and she was not used to spending money on taxis. However, over time she realized that there were some benefits to not driving. She could sit back and relax as a passenger, and she could save money by not having to maintain a car. Also, she learned that she could take her disabled parking permit with her to use for any vehicle in which she was a passenger.

Mrs. Martino was getting lonely and loathed cooking and eating by herself. Her son suggested that she contact her local health board and sign up for congregate meals. This would prevent her from being tied at home every day at noon to receive the volunteer and would also put her in contact with other people. Volunteers served the meals in an apartment common room a few blocks away from her apartment.

Because her blindness and chronic congestive heart failure prevented her from driving, Mrs. Martino qualified to use the local elder transportation service run by her health board. By making a phone call, she could book the minibus to pick her up and deliver her back to her apartment. They would also drive her to her medical or other appointments. The only problem was that she had to book the bus well in advance because it was often full.

Mrs. Martino liked eating with other people and enjoyed the good nutritious meals. When she couldn't take the elder minibus, she took a taxi. Luckily, because her physician had assessed her unable to take public transport, she qualified for taxi savers and paid only half the cost of the taxi fare.

Private home support

Mrs. Martino still swam every nice day and had visitors. With the help of her son, they found a suitable cleaning person and he and his family had her over for dinner once or twice a week. During this year, she had another congestive heart failure attack. Luckily, her apartment neighbor heard her cries and called 911. She was taken to the hospital to be stabilized for a few days, then returned home.

After the heart attack, Mrs. Martino became weaker and needed more help. Her son called a private agency to hire a home-maker to supervise the bath and make two meals daily. The homemaker also did the shopping.

Mrs. Martino was not pleased with the arrangement because she still did not like to have strangers in her apartment. She resisted any formal help and felt that her son could give her all the help she needed. Her son felt otherwise. He explained to his mother that he wanted to be a son, not a caregiver, and he felt that having to do the cleaning, grocery shopping, and preparing meals when he came to visit cut down on their time together.

After a time, Mrs. Martino came to know and trust the homemaker, and the agency assured the son that the same person would be there daily. Mrs. Martino hated paying so much for help, but luckily the private home support agency was cheaper than the government agency through the regional health board.

Environmental support facilities

As Mrs. Martino became frailer, she needed to make environmental changes to her apartment to make things easy and safe. Getting in and out of the tub was a problem, so grab bars and a hand-held shower were installed in the bath to make it safer. Her son looked at the apartment to see how barrier free it was. With a few exceptions, it was almost barrier free: the step-off platform on the balcony and the sliding door tracks to the balcony were not recessed. Her son installed a sloping cover on the raised door tracks to make the balcony accessible, and a small ramp on the raised step-off platform of the balcony allowed her to water her plants.

If the hall furniture was removed, it was wide enough for a wheelchair or walker. Neither the kitchen nor bathrooms were designed to accommodate a wheelchair. However, the master bathroom had room to transfer from a wheelchair to the toilet.

Private personal care homes

In her 87th year, Mrs. Martino was having a difficult time. She hated not being able to see, she was tired all the time, and if she did any kind of activity, she was short of breath.

She looked into a private personal care home nearby where she had some friends. Personal care homes are private, non-government-supported institutions of more than three people that provide some nursing care to clients (usually less than a half-hour per client per day). Because the facilities are private, they are usually fairly expensive.

This private facility had independent living with congregate meals. Mrs. Martino thought it would be nice to have her meals provided and a place to entertain. If she got sick, she would receive 24-hour nursing care in a special area until she got better. Unfortunately, if she deteriorated until she could not walk and was assessed at an extended care level (see Chapter 3), she would be transferred out of the facility. This meant that she would not be able to age in place.

This private home called Mrs. Martino on a number of occasions to say a room was available, but she always declined in the end. A move was just too much trouble, and her son kept assuring her that meals could be provided or whatever help she needed. As well, she thought she might be cramped in the private home because she would only be given a two-bedroom apartment.

More and more days passed when she just had to rest. She did not have the energy to go out, but if she did go to get groceries and arranged to have them delivered, she was just too tired the rest of the day. Swimming in the morning meant she had to rest several hours afterward before she had the energy to have someone to tea.

Live-in home care

Then Mrs. Martino got pneumonia. She was hospitalized in a very weak, frail state. When her son visited her in hospital, he found his mother very unhappy with the nursing. On two occasions, he observed one of the nurses abusing his mother by saying, "You don't need to go to the bathroom again! We just moved you up in bed." This prompted him to take his mother out of hospital and home to the apartment.

He had a choice: he could move his mother into a nursing facility or organize live-in home help. Having a live-in homemaker cost more than moving into a nursing facility, but he wanted his mother to age in place. So he rented a wheelchair and a commode and hired a live-in homemaker from the same agency to replace the homemaker who came daily. One homemaker lived in for five days, and a second one came on weekends.

Geriatric assessment

Mrs. Martino was deteriorating. She was depressed and she felt useless. She wanted to die. A geriatric assessment team came to the apartment and did an assessment to try to work out what was best for her. The team did assessments, made recommendations, and monitored her progress. Getting her on some antidepressants was their first priority.

(In the United States, health maintenance organizations (HMOs) and the Program for All-Inclusive Care for the Elderly (PACE) have geriatric assessment teams. In Canada, they are usually associated with a hospital and may be funded partly through the hospital and partly through the regional health board. The team, a group of professionals intent on keeping elders out of facilities, usually consists of a geriatrician, a clinical nurse specialist, a physiotherapist, a social worker, and other personnel as needed. Your physician or hospital can refer you for a geriatric assessment.)

Mrs. Martino's family and friends still visited, but she was very weak and in bed all the time, except to go to the bathroom, which was a great effort. She was too tired to even listen to the talking books, and she was not interested in food at all. The pneumonia got better, but she was still depressed, and life was just too hard. Eventually, the pneumonia returned, and Mrs. Martino died at home in her own bed with the homemaker agency woman in attendance.

Conclusion

If Mrs. Martino had had no financial resources, she may have been eligible for hospice services. These are comprehensive services for terminally ill clients and their families (see Chapter 5). However, she chose to not go into a facility and was wealthy enough to afford the care she needed to die at home. Mrs. Martino was always mentally alert, so she was able to direct her own care and express her own wishes. If she had had some dementia, her choices would have been more limited, and her children would have been more concerned with her safety. Luckily Mrs. Martino never needed any type of special care unit.

Mrs. Martino's encounters with the health care system were typical of many elders. More than 90 percent of North American elders are living in their own communities, with their families providing most of their care, and formal care as supplement or last resort. This generation tends to be fiercely independent, proud, and private, and it is difficult for them to give up this independence (e.g., by accepting home help and giving up their driver's licenses).

Mrs. Martino was fortunate that she did not need to access the public health care system much because she had many resources — money and a knowledgeable family. She was grateful that she didn't have to go through financial-means testing. In fact, she would probably rather have done without than go through that assessment.

Many elders, however, do not have the option of private home care, and they cannot think of anything to do but take themselves to the emergency ward of a nearby acute-care hospital. Elders use acute-care hospitals more than other population groups: they use 48 percent of all patient days in hospitals. Unfortunately, 20 percent of all visits to hospital emergency rooms result from adverse drug reactions among elders.

Mrs. Martino's encounters with the health system are but one example of how elders cope with their failing bodies near the end of life. The episodes to hospital became more frequent in her last years, and yet the stays were of short duration. Family was used as the first resource, followed by just a cleaning lady, until in the end, Mrs. Martino had 24-hour care. Poor elders without families are the people most at risk for being cared for in nursing homes.

How to Get in Touch with Health Care Services

The American Health Care Association suggests contacting the following resources for getting local information about nursing facilities. To get in touch with any of these health care services, check out the blue pages (government contacts) in your phone book:

* Hospital discharge planner

* Social workers

* Geriatric case manager

* State affiliate of the American Health Care Association

* Local medical society

* Eldercare Locator: Sponsored by the US Administration on Aging, this is a nationwide, toll-free service to help older adults and their caregivers find local services for elders. Call 1-800-677-1116 on weekdays between 9:00 a.m. and 8:00 p.m. EST.

* Area Agency on Aging (AOA): This is a federal agency that can provide you with a list of the long-term care choices in your state, including community services.

* Centers for Medicare and Medicaid

Services (CMS): Call their 24-hour help line in the blue pages or visit their Web site <www.medicare.gov>.

✱ State long-term care ombudsman program or health department: The long-term care ombudsman advocates for residents in nursing homes, board and care homes, and assisted-living facilities. They have state and local offices.

✱ State Health Insurance Assistance program (SHIP): These are state programs that get money from the federal government to give free health insurance counseling and assistance to people with Medicare.

✱ State Medical Assistance Office: This office gives information about state programs that help pay health and nursing home costs for people with low incomes and limited resources.

✱ State Survey Agency: This agency helps with questions or complaints about the quality of care and the quality of life in a nursing home.

To get in touch with local health care services in Canada, the health department at City Hall will usually refer you to your local health unit. Or call the local number for Health Canada (check in the federal section of the blue pages). They can tell you about nursing care accessibility across the provinces.

The federal pension department can tell you about the Income Security programs of Human Resources Development Canada and the Canada Pension Plan, including CPP disability and Old Age Security.

Don't forget to also talk to your minister, priest, rabbi, or other spiritual advisor, as well as friends and neighbors who may have had direct experience using local nursing facilities. Many facilities have individual Web sites, and if they are not too busy, your local hospital may be able to give you some information.

Chapter 3

ASSESSMENT LEVELS

Before you even consider moving into a care facility, you need to determine what level of care is the most appropriate for you. If you enter a facility that provides 24-hour nursing care when you really need assistance only with your meals and house-keeping, you are not making best use of those facilities. However, if you require constant nursing care, and the facility you are in provides only two hours of care a day, you will not be receiving sufficient care for your needs.

To be eligible for government support and admission to a Canadian nursing home, someone in the health unit — either a nurse or social worker — must assess you. In the United States, the Minimum Data Set is used to assess elders admitted to a nursing home. Medicare then out-lines what type of care and facilities are available to you and how much financial assistance you will get from them. See

Chapter 10 for more information on eligibility for admission to a nursing home.

While each country uses different terms and definitions, the principle of assessment is the same. The assessor evaluates your functional, physical, and mental abilities based on the activities of daily living (ADL) and the instrumental activities of daily living (IADL). You are then categorized according to your ability, which determines whether you are eligible for in-home help or need to be placed in a facility. An assessment can also help you choose a facility that will allow you to age in place, rather than having to move when the facility can no longer provide you with adequate care.

This chapter will look at the Canadian levels of assessment. They include —

* personal care,

* intermediate care level 1,

* intermediate care level 2,

* intermediate care level 3,

* extended care, and

* special care.

The US uses similar assessment categories. See Table 1 later in this chapter for a summary of care levels.

Personal Care

At the personal-care level, you are independently mobile, with or without mechanical aids such as a wheelchair or walking cane. You require only minimal nonprofessional assistance or supervision. You may need help with instrumental activities of daily living (see Chapter 2) such as banking or shopping, but physically and mentally you can do most things for yourself.

If you are at this level and you want to have your meals provided, housekeeping services, or social contact, you have either to contract with an agency yourself and pay for the service or admit yourself to a private facility that will cater to you. The government does not subsidize personal care.

In private facilities, personal-care clients are granted up to one hour of care per client per 24-hour period. Sixty minutes of care may include the following:

* Bed-making: 10 minutes
* Help with mobility: 10 minutes
* Medication: 10 minutes
* Bath supervision: 30 minutes

The care provided is minimal. If you need more care and cannot afford to purchase it, or family cannot do it for you,

you are at risk of getting sicker and being placed in a nursing home. Although the term used is "nursing care," in fact most of the hands-on personal care is done by resident care aides and certified nursing assistants. The registered nurse gives out medications, does treatments, oversees conferences, and ensures that resident care aides do their jobs.

Intermediate Care Level 1

In intermediate care level 1, you are independently mobile, with or without mechanical aids, and require some combination of professional and nonprofessional services. You manage well, and are proficient in most activities of daily living. You require moderate assistance with only two or three of these activities. This is usually in the form of some daily care, but you don't require 24-hour professional care or supervision. Many regional health boards no longer subsidize nursing home placement or home care for people at this level. Check with your local health board to see if you are eligible.

Intermediate Care Level 2

At intermediate care level 2, you have some difficulty with three or more activities of daily living. You require help with daily tasks such as dressing, bathing, grooming, or eating, and you may need supervision with walking. You need support in order to continue living as independently as possible. You have significant health problems that require assistance and/or the supervision of a registered nurse.

Depending on where you live, at this level of continuing care, you may be eligible for home care, but not a nursing home placement. You have slightly heavier care needs than intermediate care level 1 clients and require additional care time.

Intermediate care facilities are funded on the basis that each client needs 90 minutes of nursing care per 24-hour period. It is not much time when you need help with the following activities:

* Activity program: 5 minutes
* Bed-making: 5 minutes
* Dress: 15 minutes
* Eat: 45 minutes
* Medication: 5 minutes
* Toilet: 15 minutes

Note that there is no time for a bath within this schedule.

Because the resident care aides often have 8 to 15 clients per day and many tasks to complete, it is no wonder elders are not talked to. Also, it is more time-consuming to let an elder help dress himself or herself or get to the toilet, so activities tend to be done *for* clients, not *with* clients in most facilities. The above time estimates are based on a well elder. When the flu strikes and elders are vomiting or need bed care, resources are stretched so thin that the quality of care suffers.

Intermediate Care Level 3 (Special Care)

At the intermediate care level 3, you have difficulty with three or more activities of daily living, in addition to behavioral problems. This classification is used for clients such as Mrs. Campbell (see story later in this chapter) who have dementia-related illnesses and who exhibit severe behavioral problems on an ongoing basis. In most municipalities, you are eligible for home care and nursing home placement paid for by the government, although you are usually not eligible for extended care services.

The nursing time involved to help intermediate care level 3 clients with behavioral problems is substantial. It takes longer because they need close supervision and help getting started. Besides taking care of the activities of level 2 clients, registered nurses now need to redirect clients constantly. Clients may get lost in corridors or wander into others' rooms and take their possessions. They may ask the same question many times in one hour and demand an answer each time. Just finding the dining room for the client and having him or her stay seated throughout a meal is difficult for staff.

For nursing staff, being patient is an art that requires constant vigilance to pick up different cues that indicate a client is getting agitated and out of control. It takes persistence and skill to have these clients dressed, clean, and calm. They have the same needs as everyone, and it is a challenge to find their remaining strengths to help them maximize their abilities.

The government allotment of nursing time may be up to 150 minutes, allowing for the following activities:

* Activity program: 10 minutes
* Bed-making: 5 minutes
* Dress: 30 minutes
* Eat: 60 minutes

* Medication: 15 minutes
* Toilet: 30 minutes

Note that a bath may require up to 30 minutes once a week.

Canadian government studies show that in reality, intermediate care level 3 (special care) clients require four hours of care time. Often, the time allocated by governments for nursing facilities is not really adequate for quality care at the intermediate or the extended care levels.

Extended Care

At the extended care level, you cannot walk more than two steps and are functionally immobile without assistance. You have great difficulty with the activities of daily living and need help to walk and/or transfer in and out of bed or a chair. You have severe chronic illnesses or disabilities that necessitate 24-hour nursing care and supervision. Depending on where you live, you are probably eligible for home care and extended care facility placement paid for by the government. However, because your medical condition is stable, you do not require acute-care hospital services.

In Canada, extended care facilities are government-supported institutions of more than three persons. In the United States, they are usually private institutions. As with intermediate care level 3 elders, clients get up to 150 minutes of nursing care per 24-hour period. Even in these units, which are usually attached to a hospital, certain restrictions for admission apply because of staffing levels. For example, on a 50-bed unit, facilities may restrict the number to two for oxygen-dependent clients or those who have a gastrostomy or colostomy or those who are aggressive and have unprovoked behavior that may be a danger to self or others. Usually only one person per 50-bed unit may be admitted with a tracheotomy or on renal dialysis.

Because extended care clients cannot walk, staff require mechanical lifts to do transfers in and out of bed. To be safe, it takes two registered care aides to position a client in bed. Clients with chronic debilitating illnesses may need oxygen all the time that must be monitored. They may need to be fed through a nasogastric tube, to have their colostomy changed, or to have their tracheotomy cleaned or be on renal dialysis. These are all nursing procedures that must be done with skill and care.

Special Care

Some facilities provide special care for elders with permanent memory loss and confusion as a result of dementia, and who are at risk of wandering. These clients require a separate and supportive residential environment to meet their care needs.

Special care also refers to clients with severe disability or medical problems who need more than 150 minutes of nursing care per 24-hour period and require specialized facilities.

The Care Plan

Once you have been assessed, your health team will design a care plan that identifies all your physical, mental, emotional, cognitive, and functional needs. The care plan is usually the result of the Minimum Data Set assessment and is a collaboration by an interdisciplinary team of nursing home staff. The care plan should involve you and your family in the planning. The care plan addresses the following:

* What kind of personal and health care services you need
* What type of staff should provide those services
* How often you need the services

* What kind of equipment or supplies you need (such as a wheelchair or feeding tube)
* What kind of diet you need (if you have a special one)
* Your health goals
* How your care plan will help you reach your goal.

Each client also has an official chart used by the interdisciplinary team to record history and progress, treatments, medications, and physicians' orders. The chart is an official document and can be used in a court of law.

Registered nurses are responsible for writing down the progress of each client, both in the charts and on the care plan. It is important that clients know about their conditions and illnesses and that they are aware of what medications they are taking and any side effects. Every client has the right to know about every treatment, and it is part of the responsibility of the registered nurse to see that clients understand.

The registered nurse also coordinates teaching with the family so they are aware of conditions, and in the long run, that teaching can save nursing time, as the family can help with the care.

Table 1
A Quick Guide to Levels of Care

IC 1 = Intermediate Care Level 1   IC 3 = Intermediate Care Level 3
IC 2 = Intermediate Care Level 2   EC = Extended Care

LEVELS	IC 1	IC 2	IC 3	EC
Combative			X	X
Difficulty expressing needs	X	X	X	X
Disturbs others with antisocial habits			X	X
Has a severe disability/medical problem		X	X	X
Independently mobile with/without mechanical aids	X	X	X	

LEVELS	IC 1	IC 2	IC 3	EC
May continually wander away (eloping)			X	X
Needs considerable directional assistance		X	X	X
Needs moderate assistance with ADLs	X	X	X	X
Needs routine toileting		X	X	X
Needs some directional assistance	X	X	X	X
Occasionally misappropriates the property of others		X	X	X
Regularly incontinent of bowel or bladder		X	X	X
Requires daily professional assistance with catheters, dressings, colostomy, oxygen, etc.				X

LEVELS	IC 1	IC 2	IC 3	EC
Requires occasional physical or standby assist to mobilize		X	X	
Requires physical assist to mobilize with/without mechanical aids all the time		X		X
Requires physical assist to transfer on occasion		X		
Requires physical assist to transfer most of the time				X
Requires supervision for safe ambulating			X	
Requires therapeutic diet	X	X	X	X
Resistive		X	X	X
Unable to adapt to sensory loss	X	X	X	X

Case Study

Assessments: Mr. Brown's Story

Mr. Brown was in his 90s. He was always nicely groomed, and walked proudly and with self-assurance. After his wife died a few years ago, he moved to the same city as his daughter to be closer to her.

He lived alone in an apartment. Although he was having trouble seeing, he compensated by knowing where everything was placed in the apartment and refrigerator. He had arthritis in his knees and walked with a cane, but he hadn't slowed down. He loved people and made friends easily. He had lots of social contact through his swimming group, Scrabble, church, and daily family contacts.

Despite his physical problems, Mr. Brown was only at the **personal care level.**

As time went on, Mr. Brown needed help with the banking and cleaning, because he couldn't see well. Getting on the bus became more difficult, so he needed help with shopping. Luckily his daughter made the apartment more environmentally elder-friendly by purchasing a bath board and flexible shower; otherwise, he would have needed help with his bath.

As time went by, Mr. Brown's arthritic knees became more problematic. Although he could still play the big-lettered Scrabble, he needed help dressing because his trousers were too difficult to put on. His daughter helped with the instrumental activities of daily living, such as shopping, cleaning, washing, cooking, and paying the bills as well as with the activities of daily living, such as getting dressed.

At this time, Mr. Brown managed well on his own with some help with shopping, housekeeping, and personal care. His daughter was the caregiver. She visited every day and took him out, and made sure he had adequate nutrition. Mr. Brown was deficient in three areas of activities of daily living, and was on the edge of needing more home care.

He was able to stay in his apartment only with his daughter's help. He had now moved into **intermediate care level 1.**

One fall night when he was playing Scrabble with a friend in his apartment complex, Mr. Brown had a stroke. His friend called 911, and he was rushed to emergency. After a short period in hospital, he returned home. Although he was able to speak and walk with a walker, he was very frail.

The continuing care division of the local health unit assessed Mr. Brown in hospital as **intermediate care level 2** and assigned him a case manager. Because he had limited pension income, his health care was nearly free. Although he was not eligible for a government-supported nursing home bed, he was eligible for some home care.

Mr. Brown did not want to give up his independent lifestyle, but he needed constant help during his recovery. The stroke rehabilitation facility in his area did an initial assessment and some physiotherapy, but it was limited in space, services, and amenities and wasn't able to really prepare him for independent living.

Mr. Brown had lost a lot of weight in the hospital. His family was worried that he needed more help than they could provide, so his sister came to help look after him and be his companion. Once Mr. Brown had recovered and could look after himself with the continuing help of his daughter and family, his sister moved back home.

A month or so later, Mr. Brown had another stroke. This one was more damaging. After being stabilized in hospital, he still had some paralysis on one side, and found walking even a couple of steps difficult. He used a wheelchair for any distances of more than a few feet. He needed help to get out of bed and go to the toilet. He could dress and bathe himself only with help. He could feed himself but had no strength to prepare his own meals or do any of the instrumental activities of daily living. He could not remain in his apartment without a constant companion to help.

Mr. Brown was now assessed at an **extended care level.**

Under his municipality's program, he received five hours' daily home care on an interim basis, and the family did the rest. However, this situation was not sustainable. He needed help around the clock. The apartment was too small for two, so even if he could have afforded live-in help, he would have had to move anyway. After a family consultation and talking to his doctor as well as the continuing care program of the local health unit, he made an informed decision to move to the private nursing home nearby, where he had a number of friends. The facility was a multi-level care facility with some government-paid beds at the extended care level. This meant that if his condition deteriorated, he wouldn't have to move to a new facility and would be able to age in place. The family agreed to pay the difference for a private room, and Mr. Brown was ready to move whenever a bed came available.

On admission to the facility, Mr. Brown was very frail and found it difficult to adjust to his new environment. He knew how he wanted things done for him and was demanding in a nice way. However, he decided to make the best of his new situation, and after a few weeks he eventually accepted his new home. As he joined in the weekly activities, his health improved, and he gained weight. He still had difficulty walking but graduated to a walker for short distances. He began to go out some evenings with his daughter and attended all the family events. Now, a year later, he likes his new home and has made new friends. Mr. Brown will probably live there for the rest of his life.

Case Study

Assessments: Mrs. Campbell's Story

Ninety-year-old Mrs. Campbell lived alone in Seattle in a townhouse with stairs up to the door and a sunken living room with two steps. The kitchen, bedrooms, and bathroom were all on one floor. All the floors were carpeted, except the kitchen and bathrooms.

Although Mrs. Campbell had been thrifty her whole life, her behavior lately seemed a little eccentric. She insisted that nylons, underwear, and brassieres could be sewn and mended and that she had no need for new ones. She had beautiful clothes but she could not tell if they had spots on them. She would appear for lunch at a restaurant in an elegant white suit with stains down the lapels. She believed food should never be thrown out or wasted, but kept for future use. However, she had strange places for keeping the food – such as storing ice cream in the oven.

Mrs. Campbell loved her new white Cadillac. Unfortunately, she had macular papular degeneration of the eyes and was quite blind. She was a menace on the roads, and few friends would drive with her. However, she thought nothing of driving from Seattle to California to see her daughter with just a little rest and snack by the side of the road.

Finally, she did have a car accident: someone hit her as she backed out of her driveway. Although her in-town daughter knew her mother should not be driving, her doctor had said she could see well. Mrs. Campbell had memorized the eye chart. She got hysterically angry even at the suggestion that she stop driving. Her daughter tried taking away the car keys, but Mrs. Campbell simply phoned a locksmith to come open her car and make a new set of keys.

One morning, her daughter, who phoned and visited daily, found her mother lying on the hallway floor. Mrs. Campbell had broken her arm just above the wrist. She was taken to emergency and had a cast applied. She was to keep the arm elevated in a sling. At this point, Mrs. Campbell was assessed at **intermediate care level 3** because she had difficulty with more than three activities of daily living, along with a behavior problem due to progressive dementia.

Mrs. Campbell had sensory loss due to her blindness. Although she needed assistance, she was resistive to care and was combative, at times trying to hit her daughter. She needed considerable directional assistance because she could not find the bathroom. She was incontinent and needed toileting. She displayed antisocial habits such as locking out the help and her hysterical angry episodes with her daughter. She was a management problem because when she became a little more mobile, she wandered away.

Mrs. Campbell received home care. A physiotherapist went to the house to help with the exercises for her arm. Her daughter arranged for a homemaker to come twice a day to help her get dressed and undressed and make some meals. Unfortunately Mrs. Campbell did not accept the homemaker and fired her due to some supposed transgression. Despite her daughter's protests, she still thought she could do everything for herself.

Her arm hurt all the time because she continually used it and forgot to keep it in the sling. It took much convincing, but she finally accepted a new homemaker. The homemaker was appalled at the state of the kitchen. Bugs were flying around, and there was mold in the refrigerator. A cleaning lady was hired to clean up the kitchen.

Despite her abuse of the arm, it did heal, and the cast was removed in six weeks. Her daughter took her shopping, and she bought a much-needed pair of new pajamas. A few days later, Mrs. Campbell again fell and broke the same arm. This time, she tripped on the new pajamas, which were too long on her. Again the process of casting, providing unwanted help, and noncompliance with pain pills, exercise, and positioning continued. Her daughter was worn out. They were constantly at loggerheads.

Mrs. Campbell started to talk out loud to her late husband as if he were in the room. She did not know where she was anymore and was constantly belligerent with her daughter. Despite her increasing dementia, her family tried everything they could think of to keep her at home. She was wealthy enough to afford live-in help but would not tolerate anyone in her house. The only solution was to admit her to the special care unit of the local hospital.

The hospital special care unit to which Mrs. Campbell was admitted was not purpose-built. However, it was secure because the doors were opened only by code. Most were four-bed rooms that provided minimal privacy. Mrs. Campbell was a problem patient. She constantly picked up other people's things and took them to another room. She was combative with the nurses and resisted any kind of care, such as a bath. She never did understand where she was, and she constantly looked for people and things that were not there. She was very agitated and difficult to control. She never could find her room, even though they put an individual object beside her door for identification.

She continued to be mad at her daughter for admitting her and wanted to go home. The way the hospital cared for Mrs. Campbell was to sedate her to make her more pliable. As a result, she lay in her bed for long periods. This form of restraint is not uncommon today, because of lack of staff and training. It was here that Mrs. Campbell died after a few months, probably as a result of the sedation and the move. Unfortunately, she was not able to age in place because she was incapable of choice.

Chapter 4

OPTIONS FOR
LIVING INDEPENDENTLY

As we discussed in Chapter 1, elders today are surviving longer and living better than in the past. On the whole, they are a healthier group than they were a decade ago, and have avoided or lived through many acute illnesses. Unfortunately, however, many elders do have disabilities caused from chronic illness such as arthritis, which cannot be cured but must be managed.

Approximately 3 percent of elders use wheelchairs, while 12.5 percent use mobility aids of some sort. It is likely that the number of elders with disabilities will increase substantially over the next 40 years. They may not be able to live independently in their communities, and society must consider what kind of dwelling and care is most suitable for them.

According to US statistics, 40 percent of

nursing home clients would be better served in a less intense care environment than that in which they currently reside (i.e., an environment in which they have more autonomy and can make more personal choices). That is not to say that nursing homes do not have a place within the health system. Although they are a necessary part of the continuum of care, less expensive accommodations are viable alternatives for many elders.

These alternatives are seldom mentioned in the health system. This chapter and the following chapter will explore some of the alternate accommodation options for seniors. Knowing your options means you can make an informed choice regarding where you will live.

Case Study

Supportive Housing: Mrs. Smart's Story

Mrs. Smart had lived in her neighborhood for 60 years. When she bought her house, it was at a modest, affordable price, but over the years the value of the house had increased dramatically. Although in her 90s, Mrs. Smart walked to the local stores every day, and was well known to all the proprietors because she had worked in one store for a good part of her life. Mrs. Smart's children now lived close by. The family was very supportive, and never a day went by when Mrs. Smart was not in contact with one of her children or grandchildren, who all adored her.

Mrs. Smart had chronic osteoporosis and had been assessed by the continuing care division of her local health unit. One autumn, she broke a vertebra in her back, and a few months later, by just sitting down hard on the bed, she broke another vertebra.

Because her income was low, Mrs. Smart was eligible for free home care to help her recover. (Note that assessment is based on an individual's income tax statement and does not take into account assets such as the value of the house.) To help with bathing and dressing, Mrs. Smart had a homemaker come twice a day, morning and night. She could eat and toilet herself. The homemaker also helped with the housecleaning, shopping, and some meals. Her family did the rest.

Mrs. Smart could no longer see herself looking after the house. She had trouble managing the front entrance stairs, and her osteoporosis prevented her from walking to the stores and standing to cook and bake. With the encouragement of her children, she decided to look for an alternate place to live where she could have some support in her activities of daily living.

After much deliberation, she decided to try a private personal care facility/retirement home. With the sale of her home, she had enough money to afford this luxury. There she would have her own one-bedroom space with a living area, small kitchen, and private bathroom. Her meals would be provided twice a day in the common dining room along with the housekeeping of her private space. An area in the home provided nursing care at the intermediate care level. This feature helped Mrs. Smart make her decision, because if she got sick and needed an increased level of care, she would not have to move again. She really did not think that she would ever be sick enough either to need the extended care level or a special care unit. If she did, she would have to move to another facility.

Although this private nursing home was not in her neighborhood, she had some acquaintances who had moved there. She loved to play bridge, and looked forward to joining in the club at the home. This home also provided activities and had a bus for shopping and theater trips.

At first when Mrs. Smart moved in, she was very homesick for her own home. However, she felt so frail that she knew she could not go back. Her family was very supportive, visited her daily, and arranged to take her home with them for days at a time to ease this transition. They arranged for Mrs. Smart to take a taxi to get her hair done weekly at her regular hairdresser, allowing her to continue her community contacts.

Mrs. Smart found the nursing home lonely at first, but she slowly started to befriend some people at afternoon tea. After a little while, a few ladies welcomed her into their bridge group. After a month, she met her neighbors, and they would gather in each other's rooms for a drink before dinner. Cocktail time became an important social event. She was known to the group as Smart — a sign of acceptance. She adjusted to her supportive living environment, and she now feels it is home. The process for her to feel comfortable took six months. A year later, at her son's house, she said, "Please take me back home, now. I would rather sleep in my own bed, and I miss my friends."

Supportive Housing

Many elders choose to live in supportive housing of some kind. Supportive housing is an overall term for a space shared by two or more unrelated individuals who live together and need some added resources to aid their activities of daily living and instrumental activities of daily living to be independent. The support may be structural with environmental adaptations to make life easier, such as barrier-free design. Or it may involve having professionals to help with activities of daily living.

Supportive housing enables elders to maintain semi-independent lifestyles. In some cases, elders help each other out and do not need services or personnel. In other cases, the services of a homemaker or housekeeper are necessary to enable elders to live independently. These services may be provided by on-site staff or visiting community-resource people.

There is a wide range of supportive housing options for elders, although the choice is more limited when a person is severely handicapped or has limited financial resources.

For-profit facilities are privately owned and operated, but are licensed by their regional health board under the state or provincial government. These private nursing homes may have some government-paid beds, but most of the clients pay for accommodation, meals, and nursing care as needed. Some Medicare/Medicaid beds may be available if Medicare services have certified the facility. The facilities are eligible for operational funds, but not for direct capital construction funds. Instead, a set percentage is included in their operating budget to cover depreciation, in lieu of a capital budget.

Nonprofit or charitable facilities are owned and operated by a nonprofit society, and are also licensed by their regional health board. These facilities are eligible for both operational and capital funds, which means that a nonprofit home will probably be environmentally more pleasant than an older for-profit home, unless the latter's residents are all paying clients.

This chapter outlines the range of housing that allows elders to live independently but which does not provide care to them. Countries like Australia, New Zealand, England, Sweden, and Denmark pioneered this form of housing, and North America would do well to provide more of these alternative forms of housing for elders. In fact, research done in the United States shows that 40 percent of nursing home clients would be better served in a less intense care environment. You need to know that other options exist in your community. Because there are so few alternatives, those that exist may be already occupied and have limited access.

Supportive housing without care comes in many forms, including the following:

* Retirement villages or communities
* Congregate or subsidized senior housing
* Abbeyfield housing
* Shared supportive living housing
* Granny flats/Accessory dwelling units (ADUs)
* Smart houses
* Program of All-Inclusive Care for the Elderly (PACE)

The levels of care and facilities in these kinds of housing vary. The questionnaires in Part 2 of this book will help you evaluate the facilities in detail. However, consider the following range of choices that are available in supportive housing options:

* *Size:* Supportive housing can house anywhere from 2 to 100 people. Choose a size that is comfortable for you.

* *Cost:* Supportive housing is generally affordable for everyone, whether you are on a government pension or have private income.

* *Privacy:* The rooms in supportive housing can vary from elders sharing rooms with curtains between beds for privacy to elders having their own bedroom in an apartment for complete privacy, along with living and dining rooms and a full kitchen.

* *Services:* Some supportive housing doesn't offer any personal care services (for example, meals may be self-serve), while others offer complex personal and nursing care configurations that could include massages, pedicures, and meals in bed.

* *Amenities:* At a minimum, houses should offer barrier-free construction. Some housing, however, provides amenities such as saunas, hot pools, libraries, and billiard rooms.

* *Sponsorship:* Supportive housing may be government sponsored, nonprofit, or private (for profit).

* *Staffing:* Some supportive housing has no staff, while others employ hundreds. Staff may be professional or nonprofessional support staff, or a combination of both.

* *Resident input:* Check whether clients have any input into how the housing is run. Some supportive housing offers complete autonomy and control to the client.

Retirement Villages or Communities

Retirement villages are multiple dwellings of single-family detached or semidetached homes, townhouses, high- or low-rise apartments, or any combination of these within a designed space.

These independent private dwellings are usually governed by an elected board. The only staff paid for by the community are security and maintenance people.

Every retirement village is different. The costs vary depending on the type of accommodation, and you may have the option to rent or buy. Services and use of amenities usually have an added cost. Retirement communities can be exclusive, expensive, private, and luxurious or they can be sponsored by a charitable organization to make them affordable.

Usually, common facilities exist for recreation. In some cases, the community is self-sufficient, with all necessary amenities such as stores, library, banking, medical clinics, and even police. This type of housing enables elders to form friendships and do activities together, yet live independently. Some Arizona and California communities house thousands of people.

Congregate or Subsidized Senior Housing

Also referred to as enriched or subsidized senior housing, congregate housing provides shared accommodation and meals in a setting in which elders live independently in individual apartments or rooms. Congregate housing can be in a large complex or free standing with a large dining room for small groups of elders. At least one meal is provided and served to clients in a common area. Other housing programs may offer help with activities such as housekeeping, shopping, and laundry.

Congregate housing complexes can vary from five to hundreds of people in a huge apartment complex. The cost is usually affordable on pensions but may be very expensive in a private congregate setting. In the United States, there are state and federal programs that may help pay for elders who have low or moderate incomes.

Staffing includes the cook, helpers, and servers for the meals, or, in the larger congregate establishments, added staff for a myriad of amenities and services. Depending on the sponsorship, client input may or may not be encouraged. Usually there is an elected governing board.

Congregate housing is situated within the community and promotes successful aging. It allows you to maintain your independence by providing opportunities at meals or in the common rooms for socialization, friendship, and giving mutual support and security, plus access to extra services, such as housekeeping. This way of life is rooted in a well-established tradition of the residential hotels and boarding homes of the past.

People who choose this option want to live independently but have a stimulating social life. If they need privacy, they can close their doors. If they want companionship, they can pop into the common activity room to see who is around. Continued involvement of family and friends helps foster independence. Some elders move from a nursing home into congregate dwellings. According to the National Advisory Council on Aging, congregate housing tends to be popular with men and never-married persons.

Abbeyfield Housing

The Abbeyfield model of supportive (or congregate) housing is that of a family-like group living in a supportive house. The clients are frail but able to look after themselves. Abbeyfield housing is a response to one of the most pressing problems of our time — the increasing number of elderly people unable to live alone but who do not want or need the services of a nursing home.

The Abbeyfield concept is very simple. It comprises an affordable house (the size of which varies depending on the design) in which 7 to 12 people of retirement age live in their own private bed-sitting rooms furnished with their own things, yet share two main meals. A live-in housekeeper is usually the only staff who attends to the daily running of the house, the shopping, and preparation and serving of meals. Life in an Abbeyfield house therefore preserves privacy and independence. Yet its gently supportive domestic atmosphere provides companionship and freedom from worries and chores. The clients have input into every aspect of the running of their home, and often one or more sit on the management board of the voluntary society that sponsors their Abbeyfield house.

Abbeyfield began in England in 1956 with one house in south London. Today about 1,000 houses and some 600 societies exist throughout Great Britain. The Abbeyfield movement has also spread to the Republic of Ireland, Australia, the Netherlands, South Africa, the United States, and Canada. Each Abbeyfield house has its own society.

To start an Abbeyfield, the needs of the community or neighborhood are first assessed. Then a voluntary society sets out to develop a house and manage it (i.e., building maintenance, housekeeping services, minor health matters, and operational finances). Each sponsoring local society is a registered charity and autonomous. Affiliation with the Abbeyfield Houses Society provides ongoing information and advisory services, a model constitution and bylaws, committee structure, and funding guidelines, along with manuals on developing and running an Abbeyfield house. Recognized local societies are able to use the charitable status of the national society in order to raise funds before their own charitable status has been granted. The Abbeyfield Houses Society expects local societies to develop housing using one or more of the following approaches:

* The construction of a new house
* The renovation of an existing house
* The conversion of a nonresidential building
* The construction of an addition to an existing building

The aim of each home is to keep rents affordable. Costs range from $350 to $1,500 per month because of sponsorship and amount of money raised from the community.

In recent years, the Abbeyfield Society has developed Abbeyfield extra care homes that are slightly larger than regular congregate homes. Housing 20 clients, they provide a modest amount of intermediate level health care with one resident professional nurse and two or three paraprofessional assistants. Abbeyfield extra care homes are the trend for the future, especially in small communities where a variety of supportive living arrangements does not exist.

Home Sharing

Home sharing is defined as two or more persons unrelated by blood or marriage who pool their personal and financial resources to share living accommodation that provides both private and shared common space, such as a living room or kitchen. As a form of supportive housing, home sharing provides the opportunity for elders to live with a family or other elders. They help each other out and share the instrumental activities of daily living. If the elders need personal care and they qualify for home care, either a homemaker or their family provides the needed care.

Sponsorship may be available in some cases. If not, the clients pay. If staffing is not paid for by the government, the family caregivers provide free care. Clients can be completely autonomous if they are home sharing. If a government-sponsored family does their care, they have less decision-making input.

In the US, home sharing is a voluntary

arrangement. If it takes on care characteristics, it is considered an adult family home.

Granny Flats/Accessory Dwelling Units (ADUs)

Granny flats, in-law apartments, second units, or accessory dwelling units (ADUs) originated in Australia as detached, portable, ready-built, self-contained mini-houses, designed to be easily installed on the properties of existing residences and hooked up to the utilities of the main house. Now aberrations of the concept can mean a suite attached to the main house where the elder lives independently but in close proximity to family or friends. A granny flat has come to mean a second living space within a home or on a lot. It has a separate living and sleeping area, a place to cook, and a bathroom. The size varies from a mini-house to a self-contained suite.

All granny flats provide complete privacy for the elders. The only services are provided by the family, and amenities vary but are usually minimal. Granny flats are not sponsored by anyone, and no paid staff is involved. The elder has as much input as the family allows. One of the problems in cities is that restrictive zoning bylaws sometimes do not allow suites attached to single-family dwellings or a separate residence to be built on a lot designated for single-family dwellings.

Smart Houses

Smart houses use structural environmental adaptations to make life easier for elders. They are built with adaptability in mind. For example, the walls of today's nursery and study can be later removed to provide living space for an elderly parent. With good planning, these kinds of adaptations needn't be expensive.

Smart houses may feature automatic lights, temperature control at a maximum comfort level, and trouble sensors with an electromagnetic system. Other amenities include light sensors and automatic drape pulleys. This type of house uses high-end technology and multiple-use design to assist elders to age in place. The size of house varies according to the design. The costs are high because no sponsorship exists, and innovative high technology is expensive. Smart houses provide private independent living with no services.

Program of All-Inclusive Care for the Elderly (PACE)

Some states and some health care systems in the United States have developed inventive affordable alternatives to nursing homes. The Program of All-Inclusive Care for the Elderly (PACE) serves people with long-term care needs by providing access to the entire continuum of health care services, including preventive, primary, acute, and long-term care. A basic tenet of the PACE philosophy is that it is better for both the senior with long-term care needs and the health care system to focus on keeping the individual living as independently as possible in the community for as long as possible.

PACE is an optional benefit under Medicare and Medicaid. There are 25 PACE sites across the United States. Some communities in Canada run similar programs with multidisciplinary teams of health care professionals. Because these programs are part of the Canadian health care system, there is no charge to the client.

Chapter 5

Supportive Housing Options
with Care

Adding care to supportive housing means that you are helped by physical surroundings and personnel to manage your chronic illnesses. You may choose from a wide range of housing options.

Supportive housing with care comes in many forms, including the following:

* Family care homes
* Personal care homes/Board and group homes
* Assisted living facilities/Intermediate care homes
* Skilled nursing facilities
* Special care unit
* Extended care facilities
* Specialized facilities
* Subacute care facilities
* Private hospitals

* Hospice
* Multilevel care facilities/Continuing care retirement communities (CCRCs)

Family Care/Adult Family Homes

As private single-family residences, family care homes are managed through the regional health boards in Canada. (In the US, they are called adult family homes.) The provincial health units consider these homes part of their shared supportive living services. Designated for adults with physical and mental disabilities at the intermediate care level, they may house no more than two elders. They are an alternative to an intermediate care facility because they are government-sponsored.

The advantage for clients is that they have more control because they can just ask the family to change something they are unhappy about. These residences provide a protective, supportive family environment within a family home.

Anyone can apply to house an elder in their house, but they must meet the requirements and standards as established by the quality assurance committee of the local health board. Standards are fairly minimal, and concern the provision of nutritious meals three times a day and physical arrangements such as private rooms and a designated bathroom.

In the US, adult family homes are becoming more common. An adult family home is a privately owned residence that provides assisted living care for older or disabled adults in a home setting. Depending on the size of the residence, there may be about two to five adults living in one home. The goal is to provide a safe, supportive family environment. An adult family home must be licensed and regulated by the State. The costs for care may be covered by Medicaid or private pay.

Personal Care/Board and Group Homes

Personal care homes are Canadian private for-profit or nonprofit nongovernment-supported institutions housing more than three people. Usually, each client has a private room, but wards of four people and semiprivate spaces also exist.

Because the government does not sponsor personal care homes, elders pay for their room and all services. Although costs vary considerably, luxury homes can run as high as CDN $4,000–$12,000 per month. Small facilities have few staff, but larger ones need staff for services such as recreation workers for activity programs, registered nurses to supervise nursing care, resident care aides to do the hands-on care, cooks and kitchen workers to prepare and serve the meals, and maintenance workers.

Here, the nursing care for clients is usually less than a half-hour per client per 24-hour period. These facilities can include amenities such as swimming pools, hot tubs, billiard rooms, and libraries. It is common to have a client council in large homes in which clients have input into decision-making and can influence the administration to make changes.

Group homes in Canada usually contain two to seven elders with individual private rooms. The size of house varies according to the design. The staff is a live-in caregiver with minimal training. The services and amenities are sparse. Some Canadian group homes are supported or sponsored by the government and cater to elders with mental illness. Clients have minimal input into decision-making because the homes tend to be run on a medical model, and clients' opinions are not sought.

In the United States, board or group homes, also called adult family homes, are group living arrangements designed to meet the needs of people who cannot live independently but do not need skilled nursing home services. These facilities offer a wider range of services than many independent living options. Most provide help with some activities of daily living such as bathing and dressing.

Many US board homes do not get payment from Medicare or Medicaid. The monthly charge to stay in one of these homes is usually a percentage of the client's income, but in some cases, private long-term care insurance and medical assistance programs may help to pay.

Assisted Living Facilities/ Intermediate Care Homes

Assisted living facilities (as they are called in the United States) or intermediate care homes (as they are called in Canada) are what most people think of as nursing homes. The size varies from 3 to 500 clients.

In the United States, assisted living facilities provide help with activities of daily living and with taking medications. Clients live in their own rooms or apartment within the complex or group of buildings and some or all meals are taken together. Clients in assisted living facilities pay a regular monthly rent and then pay additional fees for the services they receive. The term assisted living may mean different things in different facilities. For example, not all facilities may have health services on site. It is important that you contact the facility and make sure they can provide you assistance to meet your needs.

In Canada, intermediate care homes come under the Residential Services Program of the continuing care division of the regional health boards, and are considered in most provinces to be part of the health care system. Because the government pays for health care, these homes are accessible to all eligible elders, who must be assessed by the health board. Eligible elders pay only the accommodation cost of $23 to $26 per day. Costs can be covered through an elder's pension plus his or her supplement, with a little left over for a comfort allowance. The government payment is minimal, providing a ward room only.

Health care in these homes is usually restricted to 1 to 1.5 hours in a 24-hour period. In all homes, a registered nurse supervises care around the clock. Resident care aides do the actual hands-on

care of bathing, toileting, walking, trans-
ferring, dressing, and feeding clients.
Bathing takes at least half an hour.
Toileting before and after meals means
at least six times a day for a total time of
half an hour. Dressing and undressing
takes at least 20 minutes, and feeding takes
another half hour. The 1.5 hours are all
used up, and still a registered nurse has
not touched or seen the client. The medications are distributed by the registered
nurse, who also does medical procedures
such as dressings, and she assesses clients
as well as directs the care provided by the
resident care aides.

Due to government rationing of health
services, personal care and IC 1 clients are
not supported by most provincial governments. Therefore, clients will find them in
the community or in private facilities.
Today, elders wait up to three years for
admission to intermediate care facilities.
Hence on admission, they are more frail
and in need of higher care levels than
previously. The designation of 1.5 hours is
not adequate for quality care.

Skilled Nursing Facilities (US)

Skilled nursing care is nursing and rehabilitative care that can be performed only

by or under the supervision of licensed and skilled medical personnel. Skilled nursing facilities in the United States provide 24-hour nursing care for chronically ill or short-term rehabilitative residents of all ages. The care is performed only by or under the supervision of licensed and skilled medical personnel. They are similar to chronic or extended care facilities in Canada, except that most are private.

Many skilled nursing facilities have some Medicare and Medicaid beds. In most states, this is the nursing home type that is licensed to provide the highest level of care. Skilled nursing facilities can be used for clients to recuperate and rehabilitate from hospital (i.e., they can be used for short stays and clients are discharged home).

Special/Dementia Care Unit

Supportive housing for elders with Alzheimer's disease is rare in North America. Few purpose-built housing complexes are built for dementia sufferers. Most Alzheimer's clients live in the community until their caregiver can no longer look after them. At that point, they must be placed in a facility, preferably one with a special care unit. A recent Canadian study found that more than 90 percent of clients in nursing homes had some kind of cognitive impairment. American statistics agreed. These findings mean that all facilities now and certainly in the future should be environmentally friendly and have specially trained staff for clients suffering from cognitive impairment.

A special/dementia care unit has special environmental features as well as special care requirements for dementia clients, for which the staff needs specific training. Dementia clients need a calm, safe and secure environment. Since they may hallucinate, lose their way within a facility, and wander into the community at large, it is important to consider location, signage, safety, comfort, and security of everything from bathrooms to arts-and-crafts areas. Items that might break, areas where people could trip, objects that could cut or burn, and location of harmful substances that could be eaten or drunk must be considered in designing and furnishing the building.

Elders with dementia tend to become more agitated with new limitations. A well-lit, tranquil, and comforting environment will help elders adapt. Dementia clients usually have reasonably good mobility. Walking can be therapeutic, so a safe walking path both inside and out is essential. Safety includes the security issue for these clients. Partial doors barring access to off-site must be eliminated because they are confusing and frustrating. Other environmental adaptations are more suitable. A doorway can be camouflaged by painting it to look like a garden or wallpapering it to look like a book-lined library with a fireplace painted on the door. Access to off-site can be a coded entry and exit pad that is too confusing for most clients to operate. A swing cover over the elevator button prevents most clients from pushing the button. A four- to six-inch removable adhesive strip across a doorway is enough to warn them not to enter that area.

The size of special care units varies from 10 clients to 60. The cost is covered by pension and supplements in a government-sponsored unit. The cost is substantial for a private facility. Although a private room would better accommodate dementia sufferers, four-bed wards are still in use because of limited government funding. Clients thus have limited privacy.

In the United States, some skilled nursing facilities specifically provide for types of diseases such as Alzheimer's. This means that their case mix is high for the number of resources they require in order to give good care. The case mix is a formulative method used in some states to determine clients' needs for health care resources within a nursing facility. The assessment is based in part on functional ability to perform activities of daily living, and medical and psychiatric diagnosis.

Extended Care Facilities

Extended care facilities are truly supportive housing at the end of the continuum. Another name is chronic care facilities in Canada. These institutions are somewhat equivalent to skilled nursing facilities in the US. The missing part in Canada is the short stay rehabilitative aspects of skilled nursing facilities. Because clients cannot walk, the allotted hours of nursing care by the government increases to 2.5 hours per client per 24-hour period. Still that allotment is unrealistic for real quality care, as you now add transfers in/out of bed and wheelchairs to the intermediate care activities. Feeding may involve tube feeds. Catheter care and other procedures may be necessary. It is poor care for staff not to encourage elders to do what they can for themselves. But letting someone dress himself or herself with a little help takes a lot longer than the staff doing it.

Extended care facilities are government-supported institutions of more than three persons, in which clients get up to 2.5 hours of nursing care per 24-hour period. The clients usually cannot walk and are classified as IC 3 or extended care level. In Canada, clients do not pay for services, because hospitals fall under the *Canada Health Act*, through which accessibility to all services is guaranteed. However, even in extended care units attached to a hospital, certain restrictions for admission usually apply because of staffing levels, (e.g., only 2 clients per 50-bed ward can be oxygen-dependent, have a gastrostomy or colostomy, be aggressive, or have unprovoked behavior that endangers self or others). Only one person per 50-bed unit may be admitted with a tracheotomy or on renal dialysis.

Specialized Facilities

Specialized facilities include some private hospitals that provide special complicated care for clients who need more than 2.5 hours of care per 24-hour period, (e.g., ventilator-dependent clients). Specialized facilities admit clients who are *not* eligible for extended care because of their specialized care needs. These include clients —

* in need of palliative care,
* in skeletal traction,
* on total parenteral nutrition,
* who are current substance misusers,
* who need intravenous therapy,
* with an active psychiatric illness (e.g., psychotic or suicidal),
* with life-threatening food allergies, and/or
* with nasogastric tubes.

Subacute Care Facilities

Subacute care facilities are found in the United States and are often in a distinct section of a skilled nursing facility. This level of care is designed for the individual who has had an acute event as a result of illness and is in need of skilled nursing or rehabilitation but does not need the intensive diagnostic or invasive procedures of a hospital. The rehabilitation is intense in these units and procedures such as complex wound care and post surgical recovery are done for clients of all ages who no longer need the level of care found in a hospital.

Private Hospitals

Private hospitals are privately owned and accommodate extended care and IC 3 clients. Private hospitals differ in size and amenities. Older hospitals have four-bed non-private wards and few amenities. Some private hospitals tend to hire staff without upgraded specialized care knowledge for the intensive levels of complicated specialized care clients. In the newer private hospitals, the cost to clients is hefty.

The care is intensive and expensive because staff must be well-trained. This type of facility follows the medical model, and clients are rarely consulted. Physicians have the final say in care requirements and procedures. See Chapter 6 for more information on the medical model.

Hospice

Hospice (or a palliative care facility) is a freestanding home-like facility, a unit within a hospital or nursing home or a community-based service that provides comprehensive services for terminally ill clients and their families. The goal of hospice organizations is to enhance the life of clients and give them the opportunity to die with dignity in their own homes or in a home-like facility while offering family-member support. Hospices typically have staff who offer medical, nursing, homemaker, home health services, respite care, and family and individual counseling. The care is generally pain control and management of symptoms related to terminal illness. Hospice care is typically offered in the last six months of life, and emphasizes comfort measures and counseling to provide social, spiritual, and physical support to the dying patient and his or her family.

In Canada, sponsorship of a hospice is usually a nonprofit or charitable society. Hospice services are often provided in the home by health professionals, but there are many nursing facilities and acute care settings that also offer hospice services. In the United States, hospice care can be covered through your insurance, although Medicare does not pay for hospice care at home. Hospice care is available in some skilled nursing facilities and acute care hospitals.

The size of hospices differs according to their design and client numbers. Some have beautiful amenities in a park-like setting. All hospices have private rooms, and clients and families have a great deal of input into the running of the home. Hospice is truly the end of the continuum of care. Aging successfully includes healthy dying, and these facilities or community services contribute to that process.

Multilevel Care Facilities/ Continuing Care Retirement Communities (CCRCs)

Multilevel care facilities accommodate all levels of care in one building. The facilities promote aging in place and accommodate elders at all stages of illness so they do not have to move from facility to facility.

Multilevel care facilities vary not only in size but also in services and amenities. Some are private, and clients pay well for the service they receive; others are fully government-sponsored; yet others are a combination. Staffing is usually comprehensive. Due to all the levels of care required, staffing is sometimes a problem with respect to specialized skills. The amount of client input is problematic depending on the sponsorship of the home and whether or not the home is governed by a medical model of care.

It is quite common these days for governments to design all new nursing homes and many established facilities as multilevel care facilities. This policy is an attempt to promote aging in place, so that clients move within the complex rather than to another facility as their care levels change. For example, some residential care facilities (intermediate and multi-level care homes) now have special care units.

In these special care units, the staff is specifically trained to care for clients with behavior problems such as wandering, aggression, and confusion caused by dementia and Alzheimer's disease. These units are usually designed so the clients cannot escape (or, to use the medical term, "elope") and yet there is enough walking space inside and outside where clients have a feeling of freedom.

Continuing care retirement communities (CCRCs) are housing communities that provide different levels of care based on the needs of the residents, from independent living apartments to skilled nursing in an affiliated nursing facility. Clients move from one setting to another based on their needs, but continue to remain a part of their community. In other words, the client is aging in place.

CCRCs in the United States require a significant payment (called an endowment or entry fee) prior to admission, then charge monthly fees. In Canada, there is no entry fee. More and more nursing homes are built on campuses that are composed of different housing, from independent apartments to supportive housing and congregate care, to intermediate care to special care to extended care and hospice. This range is the full continuum of care, and if you have the resources, you can be in a complex in which you can truly age in place and die a healthy death.

PART TWO

Finding the Home That Is Right for You

Chapter 6

GETTING QUALITY CARE

Nursing homes will always be a necessity in our society because they serve a unique and necessary function. However, a care facility should be more than just a place to live. In good nursing homes, individual client needs are a priority.

Client-Centered Care

One of the primary principles of quality care in nursing homes is client-centered care. Client-centered care means that every decision made in the nursing home considers the client's needs as the priority; and where possible, the client is an active partner in making the decision. Many administrators pay lip service to this concept, but in reality do not identify the needs of clients or share decision-making with them.

Consider the experience of one woman on being assessed for possible placement in a nursing home:

143

The battle is, who gets to define my life. I am sitting in a room where virtually everybody believes it is all right for a bunch of service people to define my life, and that, in fact, the role of government is to create more damn services . . . that will define my life. Only I can figure out how things work for me. I cannot work with a bunch of people trooping through my place, trying to decide what I need and who I am. I will spend the rest of my life . . . trying to keep them organized, trying to keep the teapot full.

— Snow, J.,
Oral Presentation to Symposium
on Long-Term Care,
December 1–2, 1990

Her words reflect the experiences of many elders in dealing with the health care system. In most cases, health care professionals are doing a good job and are trying to assess elders for the best possible solutions. However, elders need to feel included and that they are the ones making the ultimate decision about their lives. They also need to feel assured that all the different health care professionals they have encountered will talk to each other. In a client-centered environment, the woman above would not have needed to articulate this message.

One of the ways for you to check if a nursing home is truly client centered is to ask about its rules. If a facility has specific visiting hours, then it is not client-centered. For whom are the visiting hours? The answer is the staff, not the client. Clients would probably be happy to see their loved ones any time of the day or night. Set visiting hours, though they allow the staff to do their duties without having to contend with family, are not client-centered.

Another indication of a facility's client-centeredness is its accommodation of its early risers and late sleepers. Elders all have different lifestyle schedules when it comes to the time they eat meals, especially breakfast. An area in the nursing home could be set aside with food provided and staff to help serve both early risers and late sleepers.

Perhaps the most telling sign of a client-centered facility is the number of people who are discharged home to the community. For many elders, a nursing home stay need not be seen as "the end of the road." Often, nursing homes can help elders recover from an illness so that they can return home with help from their families or the community care team. A nursing home is truly client-centered when it rehabilitates an elder to a point where he or she can live independently again.

Nursing homes that follow a medical model tend not to be client-centered. In the medical model, the physician is head of the team, and all other disciplines follow his or her lead. The diagnosis, signs, and symptoms guide the care of the client, and the physician decides what is in his or her best interest. Cure is the ultimate goal of the prescribed treatment — which is difficult in cases of chronic disease that has no cure. Nursing care plans are based on problems, and the solutions tend not to involve the client or their family or even the frontline workers. True client-centered care can be achieved only by addressing the broader nonmedical causes of health — not only physical well-being but also enhanced social, emotional, and environmental well-being.

Some elders, because of chronic illness or dementia, will not return to home again because they will always need some professional care. A client-centered facility is set up in a way that allows the nursing home to become a permanent new home and community where the client can make new friends among the other clients and staff. It enhances social, emotional, physical, and spiritual well-being through such facilities as private areas set aside for religious services and walking space for clients to wander in a circular pattern inside or a similar covered area outside.

A relatively new concept called the Eden Alternative is gaining popularity in US and Canadian nursing homes. The Eden Alternative tries to normalize the facility to be more like a personal home. For example, they provide day-care centers on site so children are part of the atmosphere. There is a greenhouse and lots of gardens and plants for the clients and staff to enjoy and work in, and personal pets are encouraged. Homes that provide an Eden Alternative are very client centered.

Elder-Friendly Environments

It is important to consider whether or not your prospective nursing home has an elder-friendly environment. Look for the following signs that the nursing home is designed to optimize the quality of living for elders:

* *Environmental temperature control:* Many elders experience difficulty in maintaining their body temperature, and they generally prefer temperatures between 75 to 80 degrees Fahrenheit or 24 to 27 degrees Celsius.

* *Draught-free rooms.*

* *Availability of clean, cold drinking water:* Water should be available in all common areas and individual rooms because elders are prone to dehydration, particularly in summer.

* *Hot-water temperature control:* Keep hot water for client use under 118 degrees Fahrenheit or 48 degrees Celsius with a high-temperature-limit control to prevent burns. Loss of feeling and decreased reflex action in some elders make it a necessary safety feature.

An indoor barrier-free physical environment enhances successful aging because housing then enables elders with some degree of disability or impairment to continue to perform activities of daily living. New building designs and approaches can greatly improve mobility and independence of elders. A colorful, well-lit, and stimulating environment can provide cues needed by those adapting to sensory losses. The new technology means that many services previously available only in hospitals can now be provided in the home.

Barrier-free design includes adaptations made to living quarters to make access and use easier for people with disabilities. It is design that allows people in wheelchairs or people who have difficulty walking, bending, standing, hearing, seeing, or speaking to use all the rooms. There are no architectural obstacles or dangers such as narrow stairways, winding staircases, or slippery floors. Housing made with elders in mind must provide enough space and structural support so adaptations are cheap and easy; for example —

* all carpeting is tightly woven, is low pile, and securely fixed;

* appliance controls light up when they are on;

* there is suitable storage space for equipment such as mechanical lifts;

* chairs are fitted with spring seats to help clients stand up from a sitting position;

* lighting is easy-to-reach, with night lights in all areas;

* electrical outlets are available for re-charging of wheelchairs;

* light quality is excellent in all bathing, dining, living, and food preparation areas;

* extension cords are banned;

* furniture and fittings including mat-tresses, seating, bathroom fixtures, cup-boards, and shelving are designed for those with reduced physical strength and are wheelchair-accessible;

* lighting in the bathroom is good to aid client's ability to read medication labels;

* sound insulation is good;

* halls and doorways are wide enough for wheelchairs;

* kitchen design benefits the physically-challenged with adjustable cupboards and counters for people in wheel-chairs;

* levels in all corridors, passageways, staircases, elevators, and ramps are nonslip, free of shadows and glare, but contrast is minimal outside the bedroom;

* light switches and plugs are waist-high to eliminate the need to bend; and

* there is structural wall support for installation of grab bars to help toileting and bathing.

The cost of building a barrier-free dwelling, if implemented at the design phase, is only about 10 percent higher than building to the code regulations today. Barrier-free design promotes health because it avoids problems before they occur.

Elders involved in furnishing and decorating their own rooms maintain a sense of ownership, which enhances their ability to feel part of the community and encourages their independence and self-respect. In supportive housing, the additional safety features should be considered:

* Alarms, both visual and auditory

* Even pathways that are well-lit, slip-resistant, and wide enough for a wheelchair to turn around

* Filtered conditioned and humidified air, available all year round, with at least 10 percent fresh air to maintain moist skin and minimize health problems

* Fire extinguishers within easy reach
* Large color-coded signs of no more than seven letters identifying hazardous areas
* Flame-proof materials
* Rooms that have access to outdoors or at least to a balcony for fire escape
* Smoke detectors in all areas
* Ventilation systems that shut down automatically in case of fire

Any homes for elders should be designed and built with the following fundamental ten principles in mind:

1. Elders should be actively involved in the planning and development of housing.

2. Quality of life for elders should be of primary concern to planners, builders, and all concerned.

3. Accurate information should be provided to the elder about the housing construction and ongoing responsibilities of the tenants.

4. Independence must be encouraged by physically environmentally friendly features such as easy ramp access and easy-open, wider doorways and halls.

Independence is also enhanced by available service packages as above.

5. The structure should be adaptable to accommodate increasing disability.
6. Affordability for elders with fixed incomes must be taken into consideration.
7. Bylaws and zoning should be conducive to low noise, low traffic volume, low speeds, and amenities should be within easy walking distance.
8. Elders should be provided with a choice of housing.
9. Effective inter-governmental working relationships, including cooperation on funding, is a necessity if costs are to be kept under control, not only for building but also for tax assessments.
10. Housing/service packages with holistic, coordinated planning should be optional but available so that elders can access affordable home care services when needed, so that they can take more control over their own health.

Accreditation in the United States

In the United States, the Joint Commission on the Accreditation of Healthcare Organizations (JCAHO) is responsible for accrediting nursing homes. JCAHO is an independent, not-for-profit organization whose mission is to continuously improve the safety and quality of care provided to the public. It has developed professionally based standards and evaluates health care organizations against these benchmarks.

If a nursing home is accredited, it means that the commission has inspected the home and found that it meets certain national standards for care. The facility must be inspected at least every three years to maintain accreditation. A one- to three-year accreditation may be granted, depending on the number of areas that meet the accepted established standards. A certificate of a three-year accreditation is a signpost that this facility is a good one and is client-centered. Look for an accreditation certificate at the nursing homes you are considering. Accredited facilities are usually proud of their achievements and display their certificates in a public place.

The commission makes its findings available on its Web site <www.jcaho.org>. Before you visit a potential home, check out its report on the Web site. Then you can ask the home whether or not they have complied with the commission's findings and made changes if necessary.

The object of accreditation is to focus on what the organization actually does, and not just what it has outlined as performance expectations. However, as with many accreditation procedures, despite the best efforts of the accreditation teams, it is possible that the nursing home may have complied with all the standards in their written manuals, but may not actually have the procedures in place. It takes a very astute accreditation team to notice this.

Note that accreditation by JCAHO is not the same thing as certification or licensing. State governments oversee the licensing of nursing homes. States have a contract with centers for Medicare and Medicaid to monitor those nursing homes that want to be eligible to provide care to Medicare and Medicaid clients. The Social Security Act outlines broad minimum requirements for these homes, ranging from safe food storage and preparation to protecting residents from physical and mental abuse. The state is also responsible for investigating complaints about nursing home care.

A certified home has passed an inspection done by a state government agency. Some states require that the nursing home and the current administrator be licensed in that state. This means that they have met certain standards set by the state or local government agency. Note that Medicare and Medicaid will pay only for care that is provided in a certified home.

Accreditation in Canada

In Canada, no universally established standards or criteria exist to rate nursing homes, and the government does not rate them either. Most provincial governments have acts that regulate nursing homes. These acts set a few benchmark standards for quality care in nursing homes, as well as standards for environmental control and care. However, the legislation is minimal, and few of the standards are based on theory or research.

Accreditation, therefore, is an important process that can ensure some standardization of quality of facilities. Accreditation is governed by the Canadian Council on Health Facilities (CCHF). During the accreditation process, a nursing home is inspected by a team of professionals and compared against standards set by the CCHF. If a facility is certified or accredited, it has met most of the standards and has reached a nationally acceptable level of care. This means the home has written procedures and quality care in place at the snapshot time of the accreditors' visit to the facility.

A one- to three-year accreditation may be granted depending on the number of areas that meet the accepted established standards. A certificate of a three-year accreditation is a signpost that this facility is a good one and is client-centered. Look for an accreditation certificate at the nursing homes you are considering. Accredited facilities are usually proud of their achievements and display their certificates in a public place.

Although it is a voluntary activity initiated by nursing homes, some provinces have recommended accreditation for all nursing home facilities by a target date.

The accreditation team tries to establish an atmosphere of learning and improvement with a defined client focus. In particular, they consider how the care or service is used and received by clients and families. Canada's Accreditation 2000 outlines the following categories of care:

- * Integration of and coordination of care and service
- * Preparing for care and service
- * Assessment and planning
- * Implementation and evaluation of care and service
- * Ongoing care
- * Service and quality monitoring and improvement

In Canada, some intermediate care homes can be private, where clients pay room as well as care costs, and some private facilities have a combination of private-pay beds and government-supported beds. Regardless of whether a facility is private or public (government-sponsored), both come under the Community Care Facilities Act (CCFA), which outlines the type and level of staff required for facilities based on the number of clients, as well as minimal services and amenities.

It's important to note that the accreditation system in Canada has some flaws. Often, a facility is asked to self-assess its standard of care before the accreditors arrive, inviting input from administrators, volunteers, physicians, clients, and families. In reality, however, it is too costly in terms of personnel time to involve more than a few people in the assessment. Therefore, the assessment may not be an accurate reflection of the nursing facility.

In addition, the team of accreditors only makes recommendations for ways to come up to standard but has no say as to when this must be done, or clout as to what can happen if a facility does not meet standards. If a facility can show it is working on the problem, it is then deemed to have met the standard. The accreditors do not need to see the actual outcome, so it may never be put in place.

Chapter 7

WHO WILL BE CARING FOR YOU

This chapter gives you a glimpse behind the scenes of a nursing home. Nursing homes are a collection of individuals — not only clients, but also staff. The type and number of staff will depend on the number of clients in a facility; but generally, the number of staff (including part-time employees, as most large facilities have shift work) equals the number of clients. While this may seem like a large number of staff, in reality the staff work extremely hard to maintain care standards and perform their jobs well.

What follows is an outline of some of the positions you may find in your nursing home.

Administrator
The administrator is the ultimate authority in a nursing home and is responsible for the entire operation. The administrator hires heads of departments, oversees the maintenance and kitchen staff, and deals

with the union. He or she is also responsible for the financial viability of the facility. Some larger homes may have an assistant administrator who shares the duties with the administrator.

In charitable, nonprofit, or religious nursing facilities the administrator usually reports to a Board of Directors. In for-profit organizations, the administrator reports to the wider corporate organization. In government-supported homes the administrator reports to the health board.

Generally, an administrator is required to have a postgraduate degree in a health profession. A master's in long-term care administration is preferred.

Administration is not always an easy job. Administrators are responsible for the quality of care provided within their nursing homes, and they have to follow the guidelines established by the legislation that mandates minimum requirements to carry out that care. The story at the end of this chapter shows how administrators must weigh risk and assess how best to serve the interests of clients.

Director of Care

The director of care is in charge of everything related to client care, from hiring, educating, and scheduling the nursing staff to admitting and discharging clients. The director of care also ensures the quality of care through promoting best practice through procedures and sits on the quality assurance, infection control, and disaster planning committees.

Large nursing homes (or skilled nursing facilities in the United States) may have an assistant director of care. Duties are usually divided, with one person responsible for education, hiring, and scheduling and the other responsible for admitting and administration.

A director of care is a registered nurse, preferably with a university degree.

Registered Nurses

Registered nurses are responsible for the overall welfare of clients through assessment and evaluation of their clients' progress and conditions. They interpret the physician's orders, coordinate client care, write the care plans and charts for each client, and administer medications. They also deal with families. Registered nurses report to the director of care.

To be a registered nurse, one must take two to four years of training at a college or university. Qualification is by exam at the provincial or state level. Registered nurses belong to a professional, self-regulated association. There is no reciprocity between the United States and Canada, although there is reciprocity between individual states across the United States and individual provinces across Canada.

Nurse Practitioners

Nurse practitioners are another class of registered nurse. In Canada, they are called registered nurse extended class. The nurse practitioner has an expanded scope of practice and does physical exams and orders lab tests and drugs. They save the system money because they are not as expensive as a physician. They do the initial exam, and if something is wrong, they then refer the client to a physician.

Nurse practitioners may be independent of a facility and may, therefore, bill separately to an insurer. Larger nursing homes may have one on staff because they are less expensive than hiring a physician and may be more specifically educated to care for the elderly client.

Clinical Nurse Specialist

A clinical nurse specialist is a registered

nurse with a master's degree in nursing. The extra two to four years of education means that they are experts in their chosen fields. Their role is to solve the problems that the registered nurses cannot solve themselves. For example, a geriatric clinical nurse specialist would know what type of equipment is best for what condition (e.g., specialized mattresses). He or she would be an expert on medication and would be able to consult with the physician to prescribe treatment based on best practice research.

Clinical nurse specialists may be used as consultants in hospitals, extended care attached to a hospital, or in the community at an administrative level. Geriatric specialists tend to be rare, and for that reason they can be expensive to hire.

Resident Care Aides

Resident care aides (also called certified nurse assistants) do the hands-on personal client care. They bathe, dress, feed, and position clients and report their findings to the registered nurse.

Qualifications for resident care aides vary between states and provinces, but generally the training takes anywhere from three months to eighteen months at a college or qualified private school. There are no national qualifications required but the teaching facility must be licensed by the state or province guaranteeing the quality of their students. Because of the variation in training there is also a huge variation in quality of staff.

Dietician

Dieticians are on staff of larger nursing homes and plan the nutritional intake of all clients. They are responsible for special diets. In some homes, they hire, educate, schedule, and evaluate the chef, cook, and kitchen aides.

Their training is from two to four years at a college or university. The dietician is usually hired by and reports to the administrator. One dietician can be shared between numerous homes.

Cook

Cooks order and prepare the food. They may report to the dietician or directly to the administrator. Assisted living facilities in the United States and congregate care facilities in Canada hire a chef because it is important to them that food be well presented yet nutritious.

Cooks are college trained or from a culinary institute. The training is one to three years.

Maintenance Director

The maintenance director is hired by and reports to the administrator. He or she is responsible for the physical building and conditions of the nursing home, including heat, air conditioning, water, and light. The maintenance director is responsible for the cleanliness and physical safety of the facility and must ensure that the grounds and appliances are kept in good repair.

In large homes, maintenance workers report to the maintenance director. Other names for this position are industrial engineer or plant supervisor.

Qualifications and training for maintenance directors vary, but college and industrial training certificates are necessary. Maintenance workers also need certification from a private school or college.

Receptionist

The receptionist is usually in the front administrative office and acts as the personal assistant to the administrator. The receptionist monitors the visitors and answers the telephone and directs calls. He or she may also be responsible for payroll or distribution of mail.

Large nursing homes and skilled nursing facilities may have ward clerks. Ward clerks schedule appointments for clients, coordinate care conferences, and generally act as secretaries to the registered nurse responsible for the group of clients.

Qualifications required for receptionist and ward clerk positions depend on the size of the facility and the tasks that the person is required to perform.

Physician

Skilled nursing facilities in the United States usually have physicians on staff. In Canada, physicians are independent, although a home may have a specific physician who does most of his or her practice in that home. Some facilities may stipulate that clients can see only the physician who works with that home, not their own physician.

Pharmacist

In large nursing homes, a pharmacist distributes drugs. In smaller facilities, an off-site pharmacist administers drug blister packs.

Pharmacy is a four-year qualifying university course and is governed by a professional organization that demands regular upgrades in practice.

Social Worker
It is not unusual for a skilled nursing facility or nursing home to have a social worker on staff. That person works with families and can troubleshoot clients' nonmedical problems.

Recreation Therapist
In some states and provinces, it is mandatory for nursing homes to provide some recreation programs. The recreation therapist conducts the facility tours if there is no social worker and can be an adjunct to the physiotherapist or occupational therapist. He or she is also responsible for the facility client events, such as special parties, games, group activities, outings, or music therapy if there is no designated music therapist.

A recreation therapist must have some qualification from a college or private school. The course varies from six months to two years in length. There is no professional organization so the quality of personnel varies greatly, as does the quality of programming.

Other Staff

Other full- or part-time facility staff members may include —

* chaplain, minister, priest, rabbi, or other spiritual advisors;
* physiotherapist;
* occupational therapist;
* massage therapist;
* podiatrist;
* dentist;
* hygienist; and/or
* respiratory or speech therapist.

Case Study

A Day in the Life of an Administrator: Sally King's Story

It was a clear, crisp autumn morning. This was to be a special day: Sunny Acres was getting ready for the accreditation team. Getting ready for the accreditors took months of preparation, and four consultants had been brought in to help with the process. They were in an all-day off-site meeting with the home's administrators (director of care, assistant director, dietician, housekeeper, and maintenance heads) to make sure procedures, policies, charts, and care plans were in order. One consultant, Sally King, who had been at the home for a few months, was to be acting administrator for the day.

Sunny Acres was a big home of about 350 clients, and Sally was terrified something would go wrong. She arrived early at work on this day. It was 6:30 a.m., and all was well. She took the elevator up to the top floor to make her first walk-through for the day. She met briefly with all the registered nurses on each of the four floors and told them she had great confidence in their leadership abilities, and she was certain they could handle anything untoward. She told all the resident care aides, housekeepers, and dietary staff she met that she needed their help to make things go smoothly. She then headed for the administrator's office where she would work for the day.

A few months ago, Sunny Acres had gone through some labor problems. The union for the resident care aides had received weekly complaints because of erratic staffing problems. Sally had spent the last few months dealing with the problems. There had never been a staffing clerk. Also, there was not enough casual staff to cover the regular staff's time off. Last-minute calls to an agency to provide staff were common. This was not good for continuity of client care, and it was expensive. Another problem was that union seniority was being disregarded when extra staff was needed, which led to a lot of hard feelings among members and complaints to the union. Resident care aides paid high union dues, and seniority was important to them.

The animosity among resident care aides meant they would not help each other, which was detrimental to client care. Sally had spent much time on the different floors helping them out before she had found the root cause of their problems. They thought the administration was against them, and no one had asked their opinions about the problem or the solution. They had begun to like Sally because she even helped out making beds or getting things for clients when she was on the floors. They came to her with their problems because her door was always open.

After identifying the problem, Sally had initiated a new staffing pattern based on seniority. Then she had hired a staffing clerk and more casual staff; now they had no need for last-minute expensive agency personnel. She also established an orientation program for all staff. On this day, the staff were happier than before, and care was improving.

Sunny Acres had also had financial problems due to some clients not paying their bills. They currently had $50,000 outstanding debt from clients not paying their extra room costs. Sally was slowly contacting the delinquent relatives and those with powers of attorney to collect the outstanding amounts.

The administrator's office was right inside the front automatic sliding double doors. By 8:00 a.m., Sally was back in her office starting to make the debt collection phone calls. A few minutes later, one of Sunny Acres' clients, Mrs. Quan, came into her office. Mrs. Quan was confused and could not find the dining room, so Sally gently accompanied her to the dining room for breakfast. After breakfast, Mr. Svenson appeared in her doorway. He was upset that the eggs had been cold, and the toast was soggy. She assured him that she would send the dietician to see him and would personally check if a problem had occurred with the steam tray. She escorted Mr. Svenson back to the lounge and made her way to the kitchen to leave a note for the dietician to see him. The steam trays had been defective that morning, but the head cook had already contacted maintenance to have them fixed. Another tray was being put into service for lunch. Sally found Mr. Svenson, thanked him for reporting the problem, and told him that a new tray would ensure that his lunch would not be cold. The rest of the morning was amazingly calm and uninterrupted.

Sally toured the floors again after lunch, and all was well. The nurses in charge of each floor reported that they had no immediate troubles. At 3:00 p.m there was a change of shift, and new nurses streamed in the front door along with resident care aides. Just before shift change, she heard the receptionist saying, "Mrs. Risinsky, do not go out there." Sally looked out of her office just in time to see a woman in a green coat going out the second sliding door onto the paved entrance way. The receptionist, who knew Mrs. Risinsky was not supposed to be wandering outside, followed her out but could not entice her back. Sally rushed out to help. She told the receptionist to go back, call the floor where Mrs. Risinsky resided, and fetch a resident care aide who knew her.

In the meantime, Sally, in high heels and a suit, had trouble catching up but finally came abreast of the woman about a block away. This was a busy four-lane street, and Mrs. Risinsky was just about to step off the curb to cross against a red light. Sally tried to talk to her, but Mrs. Risinsky spoke very broken English. As Sally grabbed her arm trying to turn her towards her, Mrs. Risinsky took a swing at Sally with her purse and was ineffectually but furiously beating Sally. Sally was ducking the blows as cars at the stop light started to honk their horns. Sally could do nothing to stop her from crossing the street; she could only follow.

Finally, after a few more blocks with Sally trailing behind Mrs. Risinsky, a resident care aide arrived in her car. She pulled up beside them and tried to entice Mrs. Risinsky to get into the car with her, with no success. All this time, Mrs. Risinsky had been muttering something in broken English about money. Sally suspected that she was headed for the mall, and probably the bank. She told the resident care aide to follow Mrs. Risinsky, while Sally returned to Sunny Acres to phone the police for help and to find someone there who knew how to speak Mrs. Risinsky's language.

Sally told the police she thought Mrs. Risinsky was headed for the bank at the mall about a mile away. The resident care aide who had followed her later told Sally that the bank clerks were cowering in fright behind their counters as Mrs. Risinsky frantically shook her fist and waved her purse, berating them in a Slavic language.

When the policeman saw the commotion going on inside the bank, he motioned to the resident care aide to come out to him. He asked her what Mrs. Risinsky's first name was. "Olga," replied the resident care aide. The policeman wiped his hands on the side of his pants, opened his vest, swung both of the bank's glass doors open, and strode purposely toward Mrs. Risinsky, his arms outstretched. "Olga," he cried, "how wonderful to see you." She fell into his embrace and willingly got into the police car. As she entered the front doors of the nursing home holding the arm of the police officer, she had a beatific smile on her face. He escorted her to her room, and her coat was stored safely out of sight.

Although Mrs. Risinsky was home and all was well, Sally's job had just begun. Many questions surfaced. Was Mrs. Risinsky mentally competent? Why had she left the home? How could they prevent it from happening again? If Mrs. Risinsky was mentally competent and had resisted the policeman, he would have had no right to take her back to the nursing home. Luckily Mrs. Risinsky had gone willingly, partially due to the policeman's skill in handling the situation. The psychiatrist on call examined Mrs. Risinsky and declared her competent. She could not be detained in any way. She was free to leave the nursing home.

Sally knew that the nursing home staff should have known more about Mrs. Risinsky on admission. They should have known that she was mentally competent, but that her spoken English was poor. Sally read her admission data on the chart and found that Mrs. Risinsky had been admitted three months ago in a dehydrated, mal-nourished, confused state when she had the flu. The flu symptoms were long gone, and Mrs. Risinsky seemed to adjust to her new room and new life. She seemed to be in quite good shape physically, and was certainly capable of walking long dis-tances. She did not need to be there for any medical reason. She was inappropriately placed because she was physically well now.

Sally wanted to know what had made her act out so strongly. Through an interpreter, she discovered that Mrs. Risinsky had no family in the United States, except for a cousin in Florida. She had given the power of attorney over her financial affairs to a couple in her apartment block. Unfortunately, this couple had never contacted her since she had been admitted to the nursing home months ago, and she was worried about her apartment and the money she had in the bank.

That day she had received a phone call from her cousin in Florida. The cousin, who had not known about Mrs. Risinsky being sick, had been trying to contact her for months. The apartment phone had gone unanswered; then it had been disconnected. The cousin called the phone company to find out where the final phone bill had been sent and discovered the name of the couple who had befriended Mrs. Risinsky. She tried to contact them, but they had an unlisted phone number. Through the address listed on the last bill, the cousin then contacted the apartment manager. She learned that Mrs. Risinsky was in a nursing home. On further investigation, it was discovered that the couple had sold all her furnishings in the apartment and had absconded with all her money. They had moved away and bought a house with their ill-gotten gains. This was now a police matter.

Mrs. Risinsky had every reason to be concerned about her money. She had no money in the bank and nowhere to go to except the nursing home. She was a victim of criminal financial abuse. Mrs. Risinsky needed assurance that the police were now investigating the theft of her money, and that in due process, she would probably be reimbursed for her losses. She would have to stay in the nursing home for the moment, but everything would be done to help her return to the community.

By now, it was 8:00 p.m. Sally had done the investigation, and the paperwork was started for the administrator to pick up the pieces. She had had no meetings, no labor problems, no deaths, no outbreak of infections. This had been a long, though relatively easy day in the life of an administrator.

Chapter 8

CHOOSING A NURSING HOME

Now that you have determined what kind of care you need, it's time to start the search for a nursing home that is right for you or your loved one. You'll want to visit a couple of the facilities in your community to get a feel for what you like and what you don't like. Talk to your doctor or regional health board about what facilities are available in your area. Check out your community newspaper. Some nursing homes advertise the activities they are hosting. By attending these, you can get a good idea of what the facility is like. Ask people you know for recommendations. Many people have friends, parents, or grandparents in nursing homes and they can help you narrow your search.

Once you have a couple of homes on your list, it's time to pay a visit. Make an appointment with the intake coordinator, who will take you on a guided tour of the facilities and will be able to answer your questions. He or she will probably also give you an information package to take home and read with your family. Consider going in person to the facility to make the appointment, rather than phoning. That way, you can get a glimpse of what it is like on a regular day, and not be influenced by the "sales pitch" of the intake coordinator.

The most common questions people ask when choosing a nursing home are "Where is the facility located?", "Is it near where I live?", "How much does it cost?", and "Can I have a private room?" Yet, for a major life decision, you ought to be asking more questions. This chapter outlines what you should look for when you tour the home, and more important, why you should look for these things. It also tells you what information to request to take away with you during that visit.

How to Use the Questionnaires

First, read this chapter and the next chapter. Then take Questionnaire 1 (Choosing a nursing home), Questionnaire 2 (Rating the care), and Questionnaire 3 (Staff ratios) with you when you tour the home, so that you can write down your observations. You may wish to make copies of the blank questionnaires so that you can use them to evaluate more than one facility.

It takes about an hour to tour the facility and make the observations outlined in the questionnaires and another hour to answer the questions.

The questionnaires have been tested in more than 20 nursing homes in the United States and Canada. Each question is based on theory and is supported by literature and Accreditation 2000 standards.

The questionnaires are easy to administer and have been written in easy-to-understand language. Answers are either Yes or No or require you to rate the facility on a scale of one to five. When you have completed the questionnaires, total the scores and use the charts to rate the nursing home. Remember, the rating is a snapshot of one visit; things may change from the time of a visit.

Note: Be careful to compare only like categories of nursing homes. For example, private personal care homes must be compared to other private personal care homes. Personal care homes do not have care components because the clientele is well and they are able to look after themselves. Therefore, it is unfair to compare these homes to an intermediate care facility with care components.

Some nursing homes may not have many amenities because they are located near numerous resources. Others provide transportation to community amenities and so the need to have them in-house is unnecessary. This means that their rating will be lower. You will probably recognize the reason for the low rating and discount it. It may be more important to have your loved one near you than to pick a facility with the highest rating.

Client-centeredness is indicative of a good nursing home and is reflected in positive answers to the questions and high ratings on the scales provided. A program, service, or amenity may be available but not used. It may not be important for you. Remember the choice is yours. It may be more important to have your loved one located in a facility near you, so you can visit more often. These questions are a guide to enable you to make an informed choice for the best place for you.

Questionnaire 1 (Choosing a nursing home) urges you to think about location, indoor and outdoor environment, and aspects of care and special care. Questionnaire 2 (Rating the care) at the end of

Chapter 9 gives you questions to ask the director of care about accessibility and types of rooms, external and indoor environments (including physical and emotional care components), policies, procedures, and staffing. Questionnaire 3 (Staff ratios) at the end of Chapter 9 helps you consider whether or not a facility has the staffing capacity to provide you with the level of care it claims it can.

The following sections correspond to the sections and questions in Questionnaire 1 (Choosing a nursing home). The * beside a question indicates intermediate care and extended care facilities.

Location

1. *Is the location of the facility near to where you live?*

2. *Is the facility located within four blocks of a shopping mall, bus, bank, library, senior's activity center, and physician's office?*

For you to age in place, the nursing home must be located near your former community and places where you want to go, such as shopping malls and places of worship.

Outdoor Environment

3. *Is the parking free and accessible for you when you have visitors?*

As you approach the facility, check to see that the parking is close to the entrance and is convenient for family and friends to visit.

4. *Is there a covered entranceway so you can enter a car without getting wet?*

A covered entrance is an asset as it keeps you from getting wet when it is raining or snowing. It is also safe because it keeps the ground dry and nonslippery.

5. *Are there well-tended gardens to soften the institutional look around the facility?*

Landscaping is important because it softens the look of the facility and provides a more homey feel. Research states that elders who look at a natural environment are healthier than those who do not.

6. *Is there a garden for clients?*

7. *Is there a garden for staff to use?*

Elders need to have the option of gardening and being able to walk in the gardens. It is also a morale boost and healthy for staff to tend their own gardens. In one nursing home, they grow vegetables. At harvest, the staff donate some of their harvest to the nursing home. Another home has a weekly market garden where clients, staff, families, and the surrounding community can purchase produce and homemade items.

8. *Is the outdoor walking space on the same level as the rooms?*

9. *Is the outdoor walking space weather protected?*

Walking as exercise is very healthy. Also, it is important to be able to walk regardless of the weather. There should be no barriers to the walking paths inside or out (e.g., door sills).

Indoor Environment: The Facility

10. *Does the home smell fresh (i.e., no smell of urine or strong disinfectant)?*

11. *Is the home clean (i.e., no visible dust, no scum in the bathrooms, no marks on walls, no build-up of wax in corners, no streaked windows)?*

These questions deal with the public areas for all clients as well as the specific individual rooms. If you smell strong disinfectant or urine or see any dirt or dust upon entering the nursing home, you need to question its care and maintenance.

12. Are the floors suitable for elders (i.e., not shiny, no glare, easily cleaned)?

Shiny floors that glare are hard on your eyes. It may not look as nice to have dull floors, but it is safer for you. Well-maintained low-pile, closely looped wall-to-wall carpet is probably the best floor covering.

13. What public rooms are available?

Facilities need to have small private spaces for you to meet with family or friends, as well as a place to worship and a large meeting hall. Nursing homes with a library, craft room, swimming pool, exercise room, billiard room, greenhouse, and sauna were built with you in mind and are able to cater to activities you like.

Personal care nursing homes are usually privately owned and operated, so each unit has its own kitchen. Intermediate or extended care nursing homes do not have private rooms with kitchens. Therefore, in these facilities, there ought to be a place where you can cook and store personal preference food.

14. Is there a nice place to smoke (i.e., an outdoor, covered, heated space)?

Smoking may be the only pleasure you have. It is your choice to smoke; you know the risks. Therefore, a nice place must be provided where you can enjoy a cigarette.

15. What amenities are available?

The number and types of amenities such as a large-screen TV also indicate that the nursing home is providing for your needs and wants.

16. Is the furniture in the public areas sturdy, comfortable, and attractive?

The furniture in public areas must be elder-friendly in design and covering (i.e., firm chairs a little higher than normal, with arms that extend to the edge of the seat). This makes getting up easier. Coverings must be nonporous material but not plastic, because it is sticky and unattractive.

*17. Are there handrails down both sides of the hallways?

There must be handrails down both sides of the hallways. Frail people need to hold on to something. Having a railing on just one side of the hall is not safe.

18. Is indoor walking space on the same level as the rooms (i.e., no sill at the entrance)?

19. Are there no barriers to access (i.e., do all outside doors open automatically)?

These questions apply to a barrier-free indoor environment. Some elders have difficulty seeing objects in their way and stepping high enough to walk over them (e.g., door sills). It is better not to have barriers. Opening a heavy door from the outside can be difficult for frail elders and almost impossible for someone in a wheelchair. All doors to the outside must open automatically either by the push of a button or with an automatic eye.

Indoor Environment: Individual Rooms

*20. Do the rooms look personalized and individual (e.g., do they have family pictures and personal furniture)?

Can you paint the room the color you want? Can you put holes in the wall to hang pictures? Ask questions, and check the room you are shown to see if it looks like it belongs to an actual client.

*21. Is the room furniture provided sturdy, comfortable, and attractive?

Furniture provided for your room ought to have the same qualities as the public room furniture. The bed must have automatic controls but look like any other bed. It is important that the dresser, side table, wardrobe, and chair are solid with rounded corners so you cannot topple them or be scraped by their hard edges if you fall against them. In personal care facilities, you furnish your own rooms completely.

*22. Can you see into the room when the door is closed?

In intermediate and extended care facilities, having a glass panel beside the door means you may close the door. You can be private but the staff can check on you without disturbing you. A curtain drawn across the glass gives you total privacy. In newer homes, a visual and auditory monitoring system can be used on occasion to protect your well-being.

23. Can more than one season of clothes be stored in the closet? (Six feet/1.8 meters is the minimum width needed.)

Many nursing homes do not provide enough personal space for possessions. The size of the individual closet space indicates the amount of personal space built for each client, and is an indicator of his or her worth to the builders and owners.

Care Aspects

24. *Are the nursing home's philosophy and mission statements displayed for easy reading?*

The nursing home's mission statement displayed on the front entrance wall must state client rights as well as the central focus of the nursing home. Look for language that suggests that the client is the facility's first priority. The statement must address all aspects of an individual — including physical, social, spiritual, and emotional needs. Every mission statement must encourage autonomy and independence, and thereby provide dignity to clients. When you see this statement, you know this home is trying to be client centered.

*25. *Can a resident care aide tell you the mission of this facility?*

It is one thing to have the statement dis-

190

played; another to find out if the staff knows what it says. Resident care aides who give hands-on care are the ones with whom you will mainly be in contact. So it is important to ask one of them to explain the philosophy of this facility.

26. *Do clients look well groomed (i.e., are they wearing the same shoes, is their hair brushed, have they shaved, are they wearing lipstick)?*

27. *Do clients look well rested and alert (i.e., not slumped in their chairs or with their heads on tables)?*

28. *Do the clients look happy and occupied (i.e., not staring into space)?*

These questions indicate what you should look for when you observe the people in a nursing home. If they are not all well groomed, alert, happy, and occupied, you have to question why. Is there sufficient staff? Is the activity coordinator competent?

29. *Does the staff address clients nicely and kindly and sometimes touch them when they pass?*

It is important to look at how the staff talks to clients. Sometimes they may be the client's only family. They must not only address clients appropriately, but also touch them. Seeing a staff member crouch down at eye level to speak with a client is a good sign: once again, this signals a client-centered approach.

30. Are call bells answered quickly while you are there? Time them to be sure.

You can check this out by noting how many lights are on down a corridor or by listening to the buzzing sound from someone pushing the call bell for help. If call bells are not answered within a minute, it could indicate a staff shortage.

31. Is the staff gathered around the nursing desk?

Every facility that has developed its own culture should tell you the client comes first. Staff gathered around the nursing station indicates they are not spending time with clients. The only appropriate time for staff to be gathered around the nursing station is at the change of shift, when assignments are given out and changes in clients' conditions are discussed.

32. Can a resident care aide show you where the care plans are?

33. Are the care plans easily accessible?

A client care plan is a plan designed to meet all a client's identified physical, mental, emotional, cognitive, and functional needs. The care plan is generally the result of the Minimum Data Set assessment and is done collaboratively by an interdisciplinary team of nursing home staff. In most nursing homes, the problems are outlined in one column, the solutions in another, and the date at which the solution should be reached in the third column. The fourth column is the person or group responsible for the improvement.

Client centeredness demands that the strengths of the client be the focus of care, not his or her problems. Solutions should involve client strengths, and there should be a measurement of improvement or statement of the goal. For example, for a client with chronic disease, the goal may be to maintain the same level of activity. That would be an improvement for a client with a chronic disease that is in decline. Clients have the right and should attend the conferences when the care plan is being decided by the team. The family should also be involved in that process.

As well, the resident care aides responsible for the hands-on care must be familiar with each client's care plan. In a well-run facility, they contribute valuable information to those care plans.

34. Is there an accessible suggestion box?

Having a suggestion box indicates that the facility is open to suggestions and change. If a home does not have an ombudsman assigned to sort out problems, clients need to be able to make complaints anonymously without fear of reprisals by using the suggestion box. Those suggestions are addressed at client and family council meetings.

35. Are there bulletin boards for monthly client education?

*36. Are there bulletin boards with a calendar for recreational activities?

*37. Check the orientation book for issues of concern to you.

There are certain things you should be told before you are admitted to any nursing home. All facilities should have an easy-to-follow, clear, concise, large-print orientation book for you to take home and read. The list in the questionnaire is only a sample of items that are not always, but ought to be in the book.

Although the orientation book lists activities and programs, it seldom tells you how to get involved and access them. Laundry is usually explained, whereas dry cleaning is not. Personal care homes have private rooms with showers and bathtubs. Conversely, in intermediate or extended care facilities, your use of special tubs is restricted. You should be aware of the restrictions.

*38. *Ask for an admission assessment form and check off the categories included.*

This applies to intermediate and extended care facilities. An admission assessment form contains an edited list of what to ask when you are admitted. Many nursing homes are very medical in their approach to clients. For example, the admission assessment uses physiological categories such as "urinary system or elimination." A medical approach looks for problems, needs, and illness and is not client centered. A medical approach does not ask about your strengths (i.e., how you have coped with your disabilities over the years?). Questions should seek to find out how you perceive your condition and what you think you need.

Special Care Aspects

Special care facilities provide care for clients with dementia and cognitive impairment, such as Alzheimer's disease and other specific psychological problems. A recent Canadian Health Survey showed that 90 percent of nursing home clients have some cognitive impairment. This means that all nursing homes ought to have some special care facilities. The following questions seek to determine whether the facility is adaptable for special-care clients.

39. *Is the home quiet (i.e., the public address system is not used excessively, staff and clients talk quietly)?*

The facility should be quiet, without the public address system blaring out unimportant messages. Cognitively impaired clients get more confused with interruption and noise. Soft music playing is fine for elevators but is not appropriate for where you live. A facility should have a calm feeling with staff talking quietly, not bellowing at each other down hallways.

The following question is especially important for clients with cognitive impairment:

*40. *Are there directional signs to help clients find their way to their rooms?*

Clients with cognitive impairment may get confused and lose their way to their rooms if everything is homogeneous and monochromatic. Large, clear directional signs make it easier and more personal to give directions to visitors. Saying "I'm in the blue hallway half-way down beside the picture of Mount Washington" is more effective than saying "I'm in Room 684" when you can barely see the numbers because they blend into the door. Some facilities have hallway interior design so that each room entrance is made to look like a different house entrance, and each corridor is a different neighborhood.

41. Is there an area provided for clients with cognitive impairment (i.e., a designated area for special care/ intermediate care level 3 clients)?

This emphasizes the need for a special place separate from the general population for special needs clients with severe dementia. They need a calm atmosphere in a confined space that is not too big and confusing and in which they can feel safe and find their way around. When clients with dementia are mixed into the general population, they can be very disruptive and disturbing to others, and it is not good for either group. In a special care area, staff are specifically trained and skilled in dealing with behavior problems.

42. Are the rooms protected from wanderers (e.g., are there physical barriers, half doors, or color design to disguise access)?

Because of the high numbers of cognitively impaired clients, all nursing homes must in some way protect your privacy.

43. Is there an orientation board with the date, day, and place?

It may not be important to some clients to know what day of the week it is, but others like to know. Clients with dementia simply need to know the date, day of the week, and where they are because they are forgetful. Some upmarket nursing homes have their own internal television stations that display this information and announce the daily activities.

44. Are provisions made in the special care unit for safe display of individual private items?

All clients, especially those with cognitive impairment, need to have their personal possessions about them to remind them of who they are. Locked glass cases can display those personal items, yet keep them secured.

*45. *Is the indoor walking space safe?*

46. *Is the indoor walking space in a circular loop for all clients?*

*47. *Is the outdoor walking space secure?*

48. *Is the outdoor walking space a circular loop for all clients?*

*49. *Are all the plants indoors and outdoors edible?*

In recognition of the numbers of clients with cognitive impairment, all nursing homes should be designed with circular pathways. These clients usually have good physical bodies and like to walk. Secure space must be small enough so they do not feel lost, yet large enough so that they feel they have purpose. They also need plants indoors and outdoors. Research states contact with nature is healthy and soothing for everyone. Because of their confusion, plants within their reach must be safe to eat.

Questionnaire 1:
Choosing a Nursing Home

The * beside a question indicates intermediate care and extended care facilities.

Location
1. **Is the location of the facility near to where you live?**
   - ____ 5 = within walking distance
   - ____ 4 = within 20 minutes' driving distance
   - ____ 3 = within 40 minutes' driving distance
   - ____ 2 = on a regular bus route
   - ____ 1 = none of the above

2. **Is the facility located within four blocks of a shopping mall, bus, bank, library, senior's activity center, and physician's office?**
   - ____ 5 = near all
   - ____ 4 = near 4 places
   - ____ 3 = near 3 places
   - ____ 2 = near 2 places
   - ____ 1 = near 1 place

Outdoor Environment
3. **Is the parking free and accessible for you when you have visitors?**

_____ 5 = always
_____ 4 = almost always
_____ 3 = sometimes
_____ 2 = almost never
_____ 1 = never

4. **Is there a covered entranceway so you can enter a car without getting wet?**
Yes ❑   No ❑

5. **Are there well-tended gardens to soften the institutional look around the facility?**
Yes ❑   No ❑

6. **Is there a garden for clients?**
Yes ❑   No ❑

7. **Is there a garden for staff to use?**
Yes ❑   No ❑

8. **Is the outdoor walking space on the same level as the rooms?**
Yes ❑   No ❑

9. **Is the outdoor walking space weather protected?**
Yes ❑   No ❑

10. **Does the home smell fresh (i.e., no smell of urine or strong disinfectant)?**
    ____ 5 = always
    ____ 4 = almost always
    ____ 3 = sometimes
    ____ 2 = almost never
    ____ 1 = never

11. **Is the home clean (i.e., no visible dust, no scum in the bathrooms, no marks on walls, no build-up of wax in corners, no streaked windows)?**
    ____ 5 = always
    ____ 4 = almost always
    ____ 3 = sometimes
    ____ 2 = almost never
    ____ 1 = never

12. **Are the floors suitable for elders (i.e., not shiny, no glare, easily cleaned)?**
    ____ 5 = always
    ____ 4 = almost always
    ____ 3 = sometimes
    ____ 2 = almost never
    ____ 1 = never

13. What public rooms are available?

PUBLIC AREAS	YES	NO
* Kitchen for cooking	❑	❑
* Kitchenette for food storage/tea	❑	❑
Billiard room	❑	❑
Chapel	❑	❑
Craft room	❑	❑
Exercise room	❑	❑
Large meeting area/ auditorium	❑	❑
Library	❑	❑
Sauna	❑	❑
Small group private room	❑	❑
Swimming pool	❑	❑

___ *5 = 10–11 rooms   ___ 5 = 8 – 9 rooms
___ 4 = 8 – 9 rooms   ___ 4 = 6 – 7 rooms
___ 3 = 6 – 7 rooms   ___ 3 = 4 – 5 rooms
___ 2 = 3 – 5 rooms   ___ 2 = 2 – 3 rooms
___ 1 = 1 – 2 rooms   ___ 1 = 1 room

14. Is there a nice place to smoke (i.e., an outdoor, covered, heated space)?

_____ 5 = always
_____ 4 = almost always
_____ 3 = sometimes
_____ 2 = almost never
_____ 1 = never

15. What amenities are available?

AMENITIES	YES	NO
CD Player	❏	❏
Fireplace	❏	❏
Large screen TV	❏	❏
Stereo	❏	❏
Video	❏	❏

_____ 5 = 5 items
_____ 4 = 4 items
_____ 3 = 3 items
_____ 2 = 2 items
_____ 1 = 1 item

16. **Is the furniture in the public areas sturdy, comfortable, and attractive?**

_____ 5 = always
_____ 4 = almost always
_____ 3 = sometimes
_____ 2 = almost never
_____ 1 = never

*17. **Are there handrails down both sides of the hallways?**
Yes ❏   No ❏

18. **Is indoor walking space on the same level as the rooms (i.e., no sill at the entrance)?**

_____ 5 = always
_____ 4 = almost always
_____ 3 = sometimes
_____ 2 = almost never
_____ 1 = never

19. **Are there no barriers to access (i.e., do all outside doors open automatically)?**

_____ 5 = 100%
_____ 4 = 80%–99%
_____ 3 = 60%–79%
_____ 2 = 40%–59%
_____ 1 = 10%–39%

Indoor Environment: Individual Rooms

*20. Do the rooms look personalized and individual (e.g., do they have family pictures and personal furniture)?

_____ 5 = always
_____ 4 = almost always
_____ 3 = sometimes
_____ 2 = almost never
_____ 1 = never

*21. Is the room furniture provided sturdy, comfortable, and attractive?

_____ 5 = always
_____ 4 = almost always
_____ 3 = sometimes
_____ 2 = almost never
_____ 1 = never

*22. Can you see into the room when the door is closed?
Yes ❏   No ❏

23. Can more than one season of clothes be stored in the closet? (Six feet/1.8 meters is the minimum width needed.)

_____ 5 = more than 6 ft/1.8 m width
_____ 4 = 5 ft/1.5 m width
_____ 3 = 4 ft/1.2 m width
_____ 2 = 3 ft/0.9 m width
_____ 1 = less than 3 ft/0.9 m width

Care Aspects

24. Are the nursing home's philosophy and mission statements displayed for easy reading?
Yes ❑   No ❑

*25. Can a resident care aide tell you the mission of this facility?
Yes ❑   No ❑

26. Do clients look well groomed (i.e., are they wearing the same shoes, is their hair brushed, have they shaved, are they wearing lipstick)?
_____ 5 = always
_____ 4 = almost always
_____ 3 = sometimes
_____ 2 = almost never
_____ 1 = never

27. Do clients look well rested and alert (i.e., not slumped in their chairs or with their heads on tables)?

_____ 5 = always
_____ 4 = almost always
_____ 3 = sometimes
_____ 2 = almost never
_____ 1 = never

28. **Do the clients look happy and occupied (i.e., not staring into space)?**
_____ 5 = always
_____ 4 = almost always
_____ 3 = sometimes
_____ 2 = almost never
_____ 1 = never

29. **Does the staff address clients nicely and kindly and sometimes touch them when they pass?**
_____ 5 = always
_____ 4 = almost always
_____ 3 = sometimes
_____ 2 = almost never
_____ 1 = never

*30. **Are call bells answered quickly when you are there? Time them to be sure.**
_____ 5 = 1 minute
_____ 4 = 2 minutes
_____ 3 = 3 minutes

_____ 2 = 4 minutes

_____ 1 = more than 5 minutes

*31. Is the staff gathered around the nursing desk?

Yes ❑   No ❑

*32. Can a resident care aide show you where the care plans are?

Yes ❑   No ❑

*33. Are the care plans easily accessible?

Yes ❑   No ❑

34. Is there an accessible suggestion box?

Yes ❑   No ❑

35. Are there bulletin boards for monthly client education?

Yes ❑   No ❑

*36. Are there bulletin boards with a calendar for recreational activities?

Yes ❑   No ❑

*37. Check the orientation book for issues of concern to you.

ORIENTATION BOOK	YES	NO
* Frequency of tub use	❏	❏
* Visitation & leaves	❏	❏
Activities & how to access them	❏	❏
How to complain of problems & to whom	❏	❏
Laundry/dry cleaning	❏	❏
Meal service rules	❏	❏
Process for connection of personal electrical equipment	❏	❏
Programs & how to get involved	❏	❏
Rules & regulations governing the facility	❏	❏
Statement of respect for the rights of others	❏	❏
Treatments available (e.g., podiatrist, dentist)	❏	❏
Is the book in large print?	❏	❏

_____ 5 = 11–12 items
_____ 4 = 9–10 items
_____ 3 = 7–8 items
_____ 2 = 4–6 items
_____ 1 = 0–3 items

*38. Ask for an admission assessment form and check off the categories included.

CATEGORIES INCLUDED	YES	NO
Client perception of quality of life	❏	❏
Client understanding of their illness	❏	❏
Eating patterns	❏	❏
Historical genetic parental influence	❏	❏
Independence	❏	❏
Learning needs	❏	❏
Lifestyle patterns	❏	❏
Personal aspirations	❏	❏
Safety & security issues	❏	❏
Self-management technique	❏	❏
Sexuality; need for intimacy & privacy	❏	❏
Symptoms including pain	❏	❏

_____ 5 = 11–12 categories
_____ 4 = 8–10 categories
_____ 3 = 5–7 categories
_____ 2 = 2–4 categories
_____ 1 = 1 category

Special Care Aspects

39. **Is the home quiet (i.e., the public address system is not used excessively, staff and clients talk quietly)?**

_____ 5 = always
_____ 4 = almost always
_____ 3 = sometimes
_____ 2 = almost never
_____ 1 = never

*40. **Are there directional signs to help clients find their way to their rooms?**

DIRECTIONAL SIGNS	YES	NO
Clocks	❏	❏
Color coding of walls (i.e., different corridors & different colors)	❏	❏
Door labels	❏	❏
Familiar music	❏	❏
Landmarks (e.g., furniture, paintings in corridors)	❏	❏
Large-faced calendar	❏	❏
Pictures of what the door represents entry into	❏	❏
Signs with large lettering	❏	❏

_____ 5 = 7–8 signs
_____ 4 = 5–6 signs
_____ 3 = 3–4 signs
_____ 2 = 2 signs
_____ 1 = 1 sign

*41. Is there an area provided for clients with cognitive impairment (i.e., a designated area for special care/intermediate care level 3 clients)?
Yes ❑   No ❑

*42. Are the rooms protected from wanderers (e.g., are there physical barriers, half doors, color design to disguise access)?
_____ 5 = always
_____ 4 = almost always
_____ 3 = sometimes
_____ 2 = almost never
_____ 1 = never

*43. Is there an orientation board with the date, day, and place?
Yes ❑   No ❑

*44. Are provisions made in the special care unit for safe display of individual private items?
Yes ❑   No ❑

*45. Is the indoor walking space safe?
Yes ❑   No ❑

46. Is the indoor walking space in a circular loop for all clients?
Yes ❑   No ❑

*47. Is the outdoor walking space secure?
Yes ❑   No ❑

48. Is the outdoor walking space a circular loop for all clients?
Yes ❑   No ❑

*49. Are all the plants indoors and outdoors edible?
Yes ❑   No ❑

How to Score

Give yourself the number you circled (from 1 to 5) and one point for each Yes answer.

The highest total score for personal care facilities is 101. The highest total score for intermediate, multilevel, or extended care facilities is 149.

Now read Chapter 9 and complete Questionnaire 2 (Rating the care) and Questionnaire 3 (Staff ratios). Add the totals from the three questionnaires to get an overall score to rate the nursing home.

Chapter 9

HOW TO RATE THE CARE

The questions in Questionnaire 1 (Choosing a nursing home) are based on the observations you will make during your tour of the nursing home. Questionnaire 2 (Rating the care) outlines questions to ask a director of care, intake coordinator, or the manager of the facility. It is an in-depth questionnaire that will help you make an informed choice.

The following sections correspond to the sections and questions in Questionnaire 2 (Rating the care), found at the end of this chapter.

Accessibility, Type, and Cost of Rooms

1. *Is there a wait list for this facility?*
2. *What type of room is available?*
3. *What is the average length of time before requests from clients to be transferred to a private room can be accommodated?*

These questions deal with availability. You need to know the cost and types of rooms available. Can you afford to stay in this facility? Not all rooms in older facilities are private, and if you want a private room, you may have to wait. Bear in mind that the waiting time is unpredictable because, in reality, you are waiting for someone to die.

At times of crisis, you may choose to go into a private (more expensive) facility and later transfer to a government-supported room. However, it is not ideal to change facilities. Research shows that the first three months of moving into a new nursing home are the most critical because you will usually go through an adjustment period, and that may have adverse effects on you.

External Environment

You need to feel safe and protected in your new home. The following questions are designed to help you evaluate not only a home's external environment, but also its ability to connect with external resources.

*4. Is the home's computer system compatible with the continuing care division of the regional health board?

5. Is the home's computer system compatible with the local hospital?

These questions indicate whether the facility has the ability to communicate quickly with other parts of the health care system. Having a compatible computer helps facilities to coordinate health care activities.

6. Check off safety and security measures.

Check to see that the facility has made environmental adaptations that make you secure.

7. Does the home have a recycling program?

8. Does the home have a policy for disposal of cytotoxic waste?

9. Is there a program established to conserve resources?

These questions indicate how the facility sustains the environment through recycling and careful disposal of radioactive drugs used in cancer therapies, and how it conserves resources.

10. How does the home participate in its surrounding community?

Does the facility have programs to involve and improve the surrounding community? Nursing homes, as part of a larger community, should stimulate clients by using their resources for the community. That involvement means the clients have more opportunity to connect with the outside world. For example, nursing homes can use their facilities (tubs) for a community bathing program or as a teaching facility for registered nurses.

11. *Does each client have a view of the garden or trees from his or her room?*

Research confirms that it is healthier for clients to feel connected with nature, so each client should have a view from his or her room.

Internal Environment: Care Components

The answers to the large number of questions about the care components of the facility will indicate whether or not this facility really has the client as its central focus. The questions are divided into physical and emotional care, although these categories sometimes overlap.

Meals

12. *Is the meal planning supervised by a dietician?*

13. *Are special diets available?*

14. *How often can clients request special foods?*

15. *Is there accommodation for early risers' meals, and are staff available at this time?*

16. *Is there accommodation for late sleepers' meals, and are staff available at this time?*

*17. *Are there flexible seating arrangements at dining tables?*

*18. *Is there a process to allow clients to change their seating?*

19. *Can breakfast or dinner be delivered to clients' rooms as requested?*

Most clients are concerned with how well and what they will eat in a facility. Meal planning needs to be done by a professional, and special diets must be available. Ordering the foods you want gives you a sense of independence and control, and is important for your emotional health. A good nursing home is able to accommodate your wishes. It is important that staff know and respect your food preferences, along with the times and places you eat. Client-centered nursing homes have programs for early risers and late sleepers. You should be able to choose your dinner companions for meals or to eat alone in your room.

Physical care

20. Are all clients seen by their physicians as needed?

Doctors' visits are rare in some facilities. Some nursing homes have a room for doctors and other professionals so that you can schedule your appointment during designated office hours just as you do in the community.

*21. Can clients be bathed every day if they so desire?

Many nursing homes bathe their clients only once a week. This may be acceptable to some but many elders prefer to bathe more often. A client-centered home makes an effort to provide staff to help you bathe when you want. The bathtub is not used much at meal times or after lunch and dinner, so that may be a good time to choose to bathe. You may have to choose a different time than you are used to to have a bath, but the home should be able to accommodate your request to bathe more often.

22. Does the home have clinical guidelines for the following programs?

This question outlines some of the most common physical problems encountered by elders, and will help you discover whether or not this facility has good programs and management for them.

23. Are the beds electric?

Electric beds are easy and safe for both clients and staff to manipulate. A client may lower the bed nearer the floor to soften a potential fall. Also, to prevent back injuries, staff may position the bed at the right height for them.

24. Do the call bells have sound differences to vary priority?

Call bells that are programmed with a difference in speed or pitch for emergency attention by staff are reassuring to clients. Clients need to know they can call for help and immediately receive care when they push the panic button. These kinds of call bells are usually in bathrooms, which are the most common place for clients to fall. Having different call bells also reassures staff, as they know that not every call is an emergency.

Emotional care

25. Has the facility participated in a benchmarked client "quality of life survey"?

A quality of life survey is a questionnaire filled out by clients asking how they view their lives in this setting. More than a satisfaction survey, it is part of the information sources that accreditors look for when they inspect a facility. The surveys used must be reliable, valid, and based on benchmarks. Ask the director of care to explain what benchmarks are used for their survey.

*26. Check off which religious services would be provided regularly, if requested.

27. Is transportation provided for all clients who wish to attend religious services in their community?

Choice of religious services must be available to you. If they are not brought into the facility, transportation must be provided so you may attend services.

28. Can clients choose to die in this facility?

Moving is a traumatic experience, and many elders fear the unknown of being transferred from one nursing home to another. If you are prepared, you are less likely to experience adverse consequences. You need to be assured that your bed will be kept for you, and that you can choose to live and die in one place.

29. Are personal pets allowed?
30. Are pets allowed to visit?
31. Is there a resident pet?

Pets are very therapeutic for clients. Patting a cat or dog or seeing fish lazily swim to and fro in a tank can be very soothing and healing.

32. Does the home have a regular newsletter that includes client contributions?

If clients are able to contribute to and communicate in a facility's newsletter, it is a good indication that they are recognized as valuable.

33. Is a private accessible mailbox available for each client?

34. *Does the client have a locked space available for valuables to which only he or she has access?*

A client-centered facility provides privacy to you as an individual. Having your own mailbox and locked space ensures that no one can tamper with your mail and valuables.

35. *Can clients personalize their rooms, including paint and wallpaper?*

It is one thing to bring a piece of furniture with you, but a truly client-focused facility will let you paint and wallpaper your room as you please.

Services, equipment, and programs

36. *Which services, equipment, and programs are available in the monthly fee, and which are provided at an extra cost?*

This question combines physical and emotional care services, equipment, and programs.

Physical care services include hairdressing, shave, massage, chiropractic, podiatry, dentist, transportation, in-service banking, occupational therapy, laundry,

dry cleaning, labeling of clothes, and immunization of clients, family, and staff. All equipment is available for physical care programs including exercise, fitness, swimming, bowling, gardening, crafts and ceramics, bingo, tai chi, bridge and card games, art, and woodworking classes. **Note:** Some of these physical programs and services also have an emotional component. For example, a bridge game is an intellectual activity as well as a social event.

The emotional care services include family and individual counseling, guest accommodation and meals, pastoral visits, memorial services, companionship, and telephone reassurance. The emotional care programs include pub night, weekly entertainment, outings, group travel, meditation classes, bible study, inter-generational programs, make and mend groups, and therapeutic recreation for bed-bound clients. The more services, equipment, and programs a facility has, the more it may cater to your wants and needs.

Policies

The facility's policies, procedures, and staffing form the internal environment that indicates its commitment to client-centered care. A policy is a written directive that guides action. Nursing homes write policies to comply with government standards. The legislation that governs nursing homes outlines the rules to ensure that standards are met. However, they are minimal and quite vague in many areas. Therefore, you must question whether or not this facility really has you as its central focus.

37. Is there a formal new-client welcoming committee, including a representative resident or family member?

The nursing home should have an assigned welcoming committee that includes a client or family member as one of the members. Although moving is traumatic at any time, your adjustment can be helped by a welcoming committee.

38. Do clients get the physician they want?

Your own physician can help you adjust to your new surroundings. It is good to keep as many familiar things and people around you as possible.

39. Is there a policy that provides for clients to administer their own medications?

If you have always given yourself medication, you may usually continue to do so. Nursing home policy should provide that choice as long as it is assured you are capable of safe practice.

40. Does the home have levels of intervention strategies, such as do not resuscitate (DNR) orders?

All nursing homes need to ensure that you are aware of and understand the different intervention levels of DNR orders so you can make informed choices (see Chapter 11). The level of intervention for every client must be stated on the care plan and chart.

41. Does the home have a least-restraint policy?

Research indicates that restraints do more harm than good and should not be used in any nursing home. Only very few, unique circumstances exist under which any restraints must be applied and then only for a very limited time. This must be policy and procedure in every nursing home. See Chapter 12 for more information on restraints.

42. Does a client sit on key decision-making committees?

43. Is there a clients' council?

*44. Was a client represented on a team for accreditation?

The answers to these questions indicate how the facility recognizes client worth. Although most nursing homes have a client council, only exceptional homes have clients represented on the key decision-making committees, including the accreditation team.

*45. Is there a family council?

Family councils are a necessity in most nursing homes today because the number of clients with cognitive impairment exceeds 80 percent.

*46. Does the home have a fund-raising committee to develop programs to raise money for home improvements, and does that committee include clients?

Because of rationing in the health care system and lack of funding to nursing homes, they often need to raise funds privately for improvements (i.e., for the physical indoor environments, improved programs, and increased number of services and updated equipment).

47. Does the home have specialized forms for admission (i.e., forms other than the Minimum Data Set or government long-term care assessment form)?

In the United States, the Minimum Data Set is used to assess clients entering a nursing home (see Chapter 10). However, each facility should have its own forms that reflect its own unique programs, services, equipment, and staffing.

48. Do the charts comply with the Medicare/Medicaid certification standards, the state licensing body standards, or the Canadian Hospital Standard Regulations?

All charts must comply, and usually do, with government regulations. Directors of care should be aware of chart discrepancies. Accreditors often do a spot check, and a well-run nursing home has total compliance.

49. Does the home have a formal process regarding which part of the client record is sent with the client on discharge or transfer?

Nursing homes should have a policy as to what part of the client record or chart is sent with the client when he or she is discharged or transferred.

*50. *When a client is transferred or discharged, can the family pick up the belongings from the room?*

If a client dies in hospital or in the nursing home, distraught families should not be rushed to retrieve belongings.

51. *Does the home have an evacuation plan?*

Every nursing home must have an evacuation plan for the safety of its clients, their families, and its staff.

*52. *Does the home have a three-year accreditation by the Joint Commission on the Accreditation of Healthcare Organizations or the Canadian Council on Health Facilities Accreditation?*

These organizations have perfected national standards for nursing homes. An accreditation award at the highest level (i.e., three years), gives clients and prospective clients some reassurance that this is a good nursing home. See Chapter 6 for more information on accreditation.

Procedures

It is one thing to have policies and another to carry out those policies through procedures. The answers to the following questions show how the policies are carried out in a particular facility.

53. *Check off what is included in client orientation.*

This item deals with the specifics of a client orientation. Because moving is difficult for most elders, good nursing homes have an in-depth orientation to make that move easy.

*54. *Is a risk-management assessment done by more than one professional other than a nursing professional within 24 hours of admission?*

*55. *Check off those professionals who are part of the interdisciplinary assessment and review process.*

When a client enters a nursing home, he or she should be assessed right away because changes in his or her condition may fluctuate or occur suddenly. A team of professionals gives an initial assessment and later a more comprehensive one. Those assessments are then translated into a unique care plan for each client.

*56. On care plans, are expected out-
comes dated for completion or
re-evaluation?

*57. On care plans, is there a desig-
nated person responsible for completion or re-evaluation of outcomes?

*58. Does the care plan emphasize the
client's strengths?

*59. Are most recent progress notes and
care plans kept together?

These questions indicate whether or
not the staff of this facility follow accreditation standards and are results oriented.
A care plan must list the strengths the
client has that will help him or her to
achieve the expected outcomes (i.e., either
maintain or improve health despite multiple diagnoses and chronic conditions).
In the medical model, the focus of assessments is the client's illness, symptoms,
and problems, not on his or her strengths
and good attributes.

Progress notes and care plans must be
kept together for quick reference because
client conditions can fluctuate.

*60. Does the facility use institutional
clothing on clients?

A truly client-centered home never puts

institutional clothing on clients, because it decreases their sense of uniqueness.

*61. Are restraints ever used on any client?

Some staff and directors of care are unaware of the definition of restraints. For example, some do not consider side rails on a bed or drugs that change behavior as restraints, but they are. Although antidepressants, anxiolytics, and neuroleptics are therapeutic drugs used to cure symptoms of mental illness, they are often prescribed to calm the client to such an extent that he or she is not a management problem for staff. Sedating clients to stop them from wandering or calling out is a dangerous practice and against human rights. Every nursing home must have and enforce a least-restraint policy and program, (e.g., no restraints of any kind, except in very unusual circumstances, for very limited periods of time). See Chapter 12 for more information on restraints.

62. Is there a formalized education program directed at clients and family to encourage health promotion and management of chronic illness?

It is important to educate clients and their families about ongoing client care. Because family members usually work during the day, care conferences should be held at convenient times. Usually conferences that are held on day shift works for staff, but not for clients.

63. Check the activities in which family participation is encouraged.

The job of the resident care aide is a lot of hard work. Families could ease the resident care aide's caseload by helping out if they were taught how to safely perform procedures. This kind of family involvement would mean that the resident care aides would have more time to look after those clients who have no family help. Family help benefits both the client and his or her family.

64. How many clients per year are discharged to their homes in the community?

The goal of every nursing home ought to be to cure clients successfully to a point where they can return home or go on to some community supportive housing. Elders all have the capacity to change and take more control over their own health.

Unfortunately, most homes do not maintain these views. A truly client-focused home has discharges and celebrates these as accomplishments.

65. *If there is no family, does staff accompany clients to their new facility?*

The health care system is quite uncoordinated. While it is preferable for elders to age in place, the resources and supportive housing are not available to make that possible for 5 percent of the population living in nursing homes. One of the problems is that nursing homes accommodate different levels of care; so if a client gets sick, he or she has to move. Having a staff member accompany the client if he or she doesn't have any family makes the move easier.

*66. *Does the home have regular audits for quality improvement or quality indicators/outcome measures (i.e., does it track statistics for risk management)?*

*67. *Is there an annual records chart audit?*

68. *Has the home's evacuation plan been practiced within the last six months?*

69. Does the home have a formalized process in place with established deadlines to address problem areas identified by accreditation?

These questions deal with administrative policy and audits that aid problem finding in a facility. A formal ongoing process is necessary for continuous quality improvement. It is one thing to have an evacuation plan but another to practice it and know it really works.

Staff policies

Staffing in a nursing home is of paramount importance to the quality of care and, therefore, the quality of life of clients. The administrator and director of care set the tone for the whole facility. They must be devoted to their work, both with clients and staff. Recent changes in staff should alert you to the possibility that something may be wrong. Good nursing homes have long-term staff and administrative personnel. This does not mean that changes are always bad, but if there has been a change in staffing, ask why.

70. Per category, what is the average sick leave taken per employee per year?

71. Per category, what is the attrition rate of employees in a year?

Increased sick time often indicates that employees are unhappy. An unhappy staff provides poor care. If the amount of sick leave is significantly more in one category of staff than another, it could indicate a management problem in that department. The attrition rate (i.e., the number of employees who leave) may indicate discontent. Due to lack of government funding, all nursing homes are short staffed.

72. Are volunteer contributions to work recognized yearly?

Volunteers provide an important role. A good nursing home values and recognizes its volunteers.

73. How long is the registered nurse staff orientation, including buddy time?

74. How long is the resident care aide orientation?

75. How long is orientation for others?

76. Are all new registered nurses and resident care aides required to have special training for dementia clients?

Each nursing home develops its own culture, and new employees must have time to learn and absorb its philosophy. The amount of time for orientation is indicative of the value the administration allots to education of staff.

77. *Are all resident care aides qualified from an accredited school?*

78. *Are resident care aides given a language-proficiency test as part of the hiring process?*

79. *Was a resident care aide represented on a team for accreditation?*

Good hiring criteria generate good staff. Good communication between staff and clients is paramount.

80. *Is there a dedicated complaints officer for clients (i.e., an ombudsman or advocate)?*

Both staff and clients need to be able to air their grievances to someone trustworthy. This person must not be biased and must have influence but not authority.

Questionnaire 2:
Rating the Care

The * beside a question indicates inter-mediate and extended care facilities.

Accessibility, Type, and Cost of Rooms

1. Is there a wait list for this facility?

    _____ 5 = more than 1 year

    _____ 4 = 6 to 12 months

    _____ 3 = 3 months

    _____ 2 = 1 month

    _____ 1 = none

2. What type of room is available?

TYPE OF ROOM	NUMBER	COST
Private with own full bathroom		
Private with own toilet & sink		
Semiprivate with shared toilet/sink		
3-bed room with shared toilet		
4-bed room with shared toilet		

TYPE OF ROOM	NUMBER	COST
4-bed room with no attached bathroom		
Respite beds		

_____ 5 = 100% private with own full bathroom

_____ 4 = 75% private with own full bathroom

_____ 3 = 50% private with own full bathroom

_____ 2 = 25% private with own full bathroom

_____ 1 = 10% private with own full bathroom

3. What is the average length of time before requests from clients to be transferred to a private room can be accommodated?

_____ 5 = 0 wait time

_____ 4 = 1 month

_____ 3 = 3 months

_____ 2 = 6 months

_____ 1 = up to a year

External Environment

*4. Is the home's computer system compatible with the continuing care division of the regional health board?

Yes ❑ No ❑

*5. Is the home's computer system compatible with the local hospital?

Yes ❑ No ❑

6. Check off safety and security measures.

SAFETY MEASURES	YES	NO
All coded alarmed entries	❑	❑
All coded alarmed stairways	❑	❑
All exits marked both auditory & visual	❑	❑
Call bell system in all rooms & bathrooms public & private	❑	❑
Delayed opener for all elevators & doors	❑	❑
Doorbell at entrance	❑	❑
Secured windows	❑	❑
Surveillance security (e.g., a TV monitor at entrances)	❑	❑

7. **Does the home have a recycling program?**
   Yes ❏   No ❏

8. **Does the home have a policy for disposal of cytotoxic waste?**
   Yes ❏   No ❏

9. **Is there a program established to conserve resources?**

PROGRAM	YES	NO
Conserving on disposable items	❏	❏
Heat control	❏	❏
Products bought for low maintenance	❏	❏
Water-temperature control	❏	❏

*10. How does the home participate in its surrounding community?

COMMUNITY PARTICIPATION	YES	NO
*Bathing program	❏	❏
Buy local food	❏	❏

COMMUNITY PARTICIPATION	YES	NO
Buy local products other than food	❏	❏
Clients speak at colleges & universities	❏	❏
Congregate meals	❏	❏
Directors of care meet to discuss nursing practice	❏	❏
Group administrator's meetings to advocate for changes in the health care system	❏	❏
Intergenerational program	❏	❏
Meals on Wheels	❏	❏
Participate in research projects	❏	❏
★Teaching facility for registered nurses	❏	❏
Teaching facility for resident care attendants	❏	❏
Teaching facility for activity aides	❏	❏
Teaching facility for maintenance workers	❏	❏
Teaching facility for others	❏	❏
Use facility for community events (e.g., polling station)	❏	❏

11. **Does each client have a view of the garden or trees from his or her room?**

____ 5 = 100%
____ 4 = 80%
____ 3 = 75%
____ 2 = 65%
____ 1 = 50%

Internal Environment: Care Components

Meals

12. **Is the meal planning supervised by a dietician?**

Yes ❏   No ❏

13. **Are special diets available?**

SPECIAL DIETS	YES	NO
Allergy	❏	❏
Low salt	❏	❏
Vegetarian	❏	❏

14. How often can clients request special foods?

_____ 5 = daily

_____ 4 = weekly

_____ 3 = monthly

_____ 2 = occasionally

_____ 1 = never

15. Is there accommodation for early risers' meals, and are staff available at this time?

_____ 5 = hot & cold food & staff available

_____ 4 = hot & cold food; no staff

_____ 3 = hot food; no staff

_____ 2 = cold food; no staff

_____ 1 = no food; no staff

16. Is there accommodation for late sleepers' meals, and are staff available at this time?

_____ 5 = hot & cold food & staff

_____ 4 = hot & cold food; no staff

_____ 3 = cold food & staff

_____ 2 = cold food; no staff

_____ 1 = no food; no staff

★17. Are there flexible seating arrangements at dining tables?

Yes ❏   No ❏

245

*18. Is there a process to allow clients to change their seating?

Yes ❑   No ❑

19. Can breakfast or dinner be delivered to clients' rooms as requested?

____ 5 = daily

____ 4 = weekly

____ 3 = monthly

____ 2 = occasionally

____ 1 = never

Physical Care

20. Are all clients seen by their physicians as needed?

Yes ❑   No ❑

*21. Can clients be bathed every day if they so desire?

____ 5 = always

____ 4 = almost always

____ 3 = sometimes

____ 2 = almost never

____ 1 = never

*22. Does the home have clinical guidelines for the following programs?

CLINICAL GUIDELINES	YES	NO
Meal management	❑	❑
Falls program	❑	❑
Incontinence program	❑	❑
Pain management	❑	❑
Wound/skin program	❑	❑

★23. Are the beds electric?

    _____ 5 = 100%
    _____ 4 = 80%
    _____ 3 = 60%
    _____ 2 = 50%
    _____ 1 = 25%

24. Do the call bells have sound difference to vary priority?

Yes ❑   No ❑

Emotional care

25. Has the facility participated in a benchmarked client "quality of life survey"?

Yes ❑   No ❑

*26. Check off which religious services would be provided regularly, if requested?

RELIGIOUS SERVICES	YES	NO
Buddhist	❏	❏
Catholic	❏	❏
Hindu	❏	❏
Jewish	❏	❏
Muslim	❏	❏
Protestant	❏	❏
Orthodox	❏	❏

27. Is transportation provided for all clients who wish to attend religious services in their community?

_____ 5 = always
_____ 4 = almost always
_____ 3 = sometimes
_____ 2 = almost never
_____ 1 = never

28. **Can clients choose to die in this facility?**
Yes ❏   No ❏

29. **Are personal pets allowed?**
Yes ❏   No ❏

30. **Are pets allowed to visit?**
Yes ❏   No ❏

31. **Is there a resident pet?**
Yes ❏   No ❏

32. **Does the home have a regular newsletter that includes client contributions?**
Yes ❏   No ❏

33. **Is a private accessible mailbox available for each client?**
Yes ❏   No ❏

34. **Does the client have a locked space available for valuables to which only he or she has access?**
Yes ❏   No ❏

35. **Can clients personalize their rooms, including paint and wallpaper?**
Yes ❏   No ❏

Services, equipment, and programs

36. Which services, equipment, and programs are available in the monthly fee, and which are provided at an extra cost?

SERVICE	Available	Cost range
Labeling of clothes & other possessions	❏	
Chiropractic	❏	
Counseling (family support)	❏	
Counseling (individual)	❏	
Dentist	❏	
Family or guest at meals	❏	
Friendly visiting or volunteer companionship service	❏	
Guest overnight accommodation	❏	
Hairdressing/cutting	❏	
Immunization program for clients	❏	

SERVICE	Available	Cost range
Immunization program for family	❏	
Immunization program for staff	❏	
In-service banking	❏	
In-service shopping	❏	
Laundry/dry clean	❏	
Laundry/wash	❏	
Massage	❏	
Memorial services	❏	
Monthly podiatry/ foot care	❏	
Occupational therapy	❏	
Pastoral visits	❏	
Shave	❏	
Telephone reassurance	❏	
Transportation	❏	

EQUIPMENT	Available	Cost range
*Bath oil	❏	
*Bath transfer equipment	❏	
*Body lotion	❏	
*Formulary drugs	❏	
*Hair shampoo	❏	
*Mechanical transfer equipment	❏	
*Mouthwash	❏	
*Non-formulary drugs	❏	
*Platform rockers	❏	
*Polygrip	❏	
*Soap	❏	
*Specialty mattresses	❏	
*Toothpaste	❏	
*Walkers	❏	

EQUIPMENT	Available	Cost range
*Wheelchairs	❑	
Hearing assists	❑	
Telephone	❑	
TV cable	❑	

PROGRAMS	Available	Cost range
* Music therapy	❑	
Art classes	❑	
Baking or cooking classes	❑	
Bible study	❑	
Bingo	❑	
Bowling	❑	
Bridge/card games	❑	
Choir	❑	
Community links/ current events discussion	❑	

PROGRAMS	Available	Cost range
Computer group	❏	
Crafts & ceramics	❏	
Entertainment/weekly/ monthly	❏	
Exercise/walking programs	❏	
Family & friends night/birthday celebration	❏	
Fitness	❏	
Gardening	❏	
Intergenerational programs	❏	
Make & mend group	❏	
Meditation classes	❏	
Organized travel groups	❏	
Outings during the day	❏	
Pub night/alcoholic beverages	❏	
Special theme parties	❏	

PROGRAMS	Available	Cost range
Swimming	❏	
Tai chi	❏	
Therapeutic recreation for bed-bound clients	❏	
Video nights	❏	
Woodworking classes	❏	

Note: To score, give each service, piece of equipment, or program one point. Add another point if the item is free.

Policies

37. **Is there a formal new-client welcoming committee, including a representative resident or family member?**
Yes ❏   No ❏

38. **Do clients get the physician they want?**
_____ 5 = always
_____ 4 = almost always
_____ 3 = sometimes
_____ 2 = almost never
_____ 1 = never

39. Is there a policy that provides for clients to administer their own medications?

Yes ❑   No ❑

★40. Does the home have levels of intervention strategies, such as do not resuscitate (DNR) orders?

Yes ❑   No ❑

★41. Does the home have a least-restraint policy?

Yes ❑   No ❑

42. Does a client sit on key decision-making committees?

COMMITTEES	YES	NO
Activities/therapeutic recreation	❑	❑
Board/governing/policies	❑	❑
Employee selection	❑	❑
Ethics	❑	❑
Financial planning	❑	❑
Food	❑	❑
Quality assurance/risk management/operations	❑	❑

43. Is there a clients' council?
Yes ❑   No ❑

*44. Was a client represented on a team for accreditation?
Yes ❑   No ❑

*45. Is there a family council?
Yes ❑   No ❑

*46. Does the home have a fund-raising committee to develop programs to raise money for home improvements, and does that committee include clients?
Yes ❑   No ❑

*47. Does the home have specialized forms for admission (i.e., forms other than the Minimum Data Set or government long-term care assessment form)?
Yes ❑   No ❑

*48. Do the charts comply with the Medicare/Medicaid certification standards, the state licensing body standards, or the Canadian Hospital Standard Regulations?
____ 5 = 100%
____ 4 = 90%

_____ 3 = 75%
_____ 2 = 60%
_____ 1 = 50%

*49. Does the home have a formal process regarding which part of the client record is sent with the client on discharge or transfer?
Yes ❏   No ❏

*50. When a client is transferred or discharged, can the family pick up the belongings from the room?
_____ 5 = whenever they feel ready
_____ 4 = by three days
_____ 3 = within 48 hours
_____ 2 = within 24 hours
_____ 1 = within 12 hours

51. Does the home have an evacuation plan?
Yes ❏   No ❏

*52. Does the home have a three-year accreditation by the Joint Commission on the Accreditation of Healthcare Organizations or the Canadian Council on Health Facilities Accreditation?
Yes ❏   No ❏

Procedures

53. **Check off what is included in client orientation.**

ORIENTATION	YES	NO
Introduction to key personnel	❏	❏
Introduction to roommates	❏	❏
Physical environment	❏	❏
Thorough review of orientation booklet	❏	❏

*54. **Is a risk-management assessment done by more than one professional other than a nursing professional within 24 hours of admission?**
Yes ❏   No ❏

*55. **Check off those professionals who are part of the interdisciplinary assessment and review process.**

PERSONNEL INVOLVED	YES	NO
Client	❏	❏
Dietician	❏	❏
Family	❏	❏
Housekeeping personnel	❏	❏
Pharmacy personnel	❏	❏
Physician	❏	❏
Physio/occupational therapist	❏	❏
RCA	❏	❏
RN	❏	❏
Social worker	❏	❏
Therapeutic recreation director	❏	❏

*56. On care plans, are expected outcomes dated for completion or re-evaluation?
Yes ❏   No ❏

*57. On care plans, is there a designated person responsible for completion or re-evaluation of outcomes?
Yes ❑   No ❑

*58. Does the care plan emphasize the client's strengths?
Yes ❑   No ❑

*59. Are most recent progress notes and care plans kept together?
Yes ❑   No ❑

*60. Does the facility use institutional clothing on clients?
_____ 5 = never
_____ 4 = sometimes
_____ 3 = monthly
_____ 2 = weekly
_____ 1 = daily

*61. Are restraints ever used on any client? Note: Give one point for every **NO** answer.

RESTRAINTS USED	YES	NO
Ankle cuffs	❏	❏
Bed rails	❏	❏
Dutch door	❏	❏
Geri-chairs	❏	❏
Isolation/seclusion	❏	❏
Lap belts	❏	❏
Poesy vest	❏	❏
Sheet & wrist restraints	❏	❏
Wheelchair trays	❏	❏
Antidepressants	❏	❏
Anxiolytics	❏	❏
Neuroleptics	❏	❏

62. **Is there a formalized education program directed at clients and family to encourage health promotion and management of chronic illness?**
Yes ❏　　　　No ❏

*63. Check the activities in which family participation is encouraged.

FAMILY PARTICIPATION	YES	NO
Bathing	❏	❏
Care conferences on day shift	❏	❏
Care conferences on evenings	❏	❏
Care conferences on weekends	❏	❏
Feeding	❏	❏
Personal care	❏	❏
Recreational activities	❏	❏
Toileting	❏	❏
Transferring	❏	❏
Walking	❏	❏

64. How many clients per year are discharged to their homes in the community?

_____ 5 = 5 clients
_____ 4 = 4 clients
_____ 3 = 3 clients
_____ 2 = 2 clients
_____ 1 = 1 client

65. **If there is no family, does staff accompany clients to their new facility?**
Yes ❑   No ❑

*66. **Does the home have regular audits for quality improvement or quality indicators/outcome measures (i.e., does it track statistics for risk management)?**
Yes ❑   No ❑

*67. **Is there an annual records chart audit?**
Yes ❑   No ❑

68. **Has the home's evacuation plan been practiced within the last six months?**
Yes ❑   No ❑

*69. **Does the home have a formalized process in place with established deadlines to address problem areas identified by accreditation?**
Yes ❑   No ❑

Staff policies

70. **Per category, what is the average sick leave taken per employee per year?**
    5 = 3 days
    4 = 5 days
    3 = 7 days
    2 = 10 days
    1 = 15 days

Category	Avg. # days sick	Rating
Administration		
Dietary		
Maintenance		
Nursing		
Resident Care Aides		
Total Rating Score		

71. Per category, what is the attrition rate of employees in a year?

5 = no people leaving
4 = 2% people leaving
3 = 5% people leaving
2 = 8% people leaving
1 = 10% people leaving

Category	% leaving per year	Rating
Administration		
Dietary		
Maintenance		
Nursing		
Resident Care Aides		
Total Rating Score		

72. Are volunteer contributions to work recognized yearly?

Yes ❑   No ❑

73. **How long is the registered nurse staff orientation, including buddy time?**
   ____ 5 = 7 days
   ____ 4 = 4 days
   ____ 3 = 2 days
   ____ 2 = 1 day
   ____ 1 = less than a day

74. **How long is the resident care aide orientation?**
   ____ 5 = 5 days
   ____ 4 = 3 days
   ____ 3 = 2 days
   ____ 2 = 1 day
   ____ 1 = less than a day

75. **How long is orientation for others?**
   ____ 5 = 3 days
   ____ 4 = 2 days
   ____ 3 = 1 day
   ____ 2 = one-half day
   ____ 1 = less than one-half day

76. **Are all new registered nurses and resident care aides required to have special training for dementia clients?**
   Yes ❏   No ❏

77. **Are all resident care aides quali-fied from an accredited school?**

___ 5 = 100%
___ 4 = 90%
___ 3 = 80%
___ 2 = 75%
___ 1 = 65%

78. **Are resident care aides given a language-proficiency test as part of the hiring process?**
Yes ❏   No ❏

79. **Was a resident care aide repre-sented on a team for accredita-tion?**
Yes ❏   No ❏

80. **Is there a dedicated complaints officer for clients (i.e., an om-budsman or advocate)?**
Yes ❏   No ❏

How to Score

Give yourself the number you circled (from 1 to 5) and one point for each Yes answer. (**Note:** For question 61, give one point for each No answer.) The highest total score for personal care facilities is 285. The highest total score for intermediate, multilevel, or extended care facilities is 423.

Now complete Questionnaire 3 (Staff ratios). Add the totals from the three questionnaires to get an overall score to rate the nursing home.

Staff Ratios

Knowing a facility's staff-to-client ratio can help you ascertain if the facility can really provide the care and services it says it does. Questionnaire 3 (Staff Ratios) outlines the optimum staff-to-client ratios, based on the experience and practice of actively working personnel. They are not the minimums that the legislation demands. A good nursing home uses its personnel well and reaches out to the regional heath board for specialized skills.

The staff ratios will depend on the level of care you require. Use the appropriate chart in Questionnaire 3 to determine a score for the staff ratios at the facilities you are visiting.

How to Score and Rate the Questionnaires

Add the scores from Questionnaires 1, 2, and 3 to get a grand total:

_____ + _____ + _____ =_____

You can then rate this total against the appropriate rating for your level of care. These ratings are found in Questionnaire 3. The higher the score, the better the facility.

Questionnaire 3:
Staff Ratios

To complete this questionnaire, you will need the assistance of the director of care of each facility you are reviewing. Find the staff ratio table for the type of facility, then circle the correct ratio for each type of professional to clients. The rating for each ratio is given in the same column as the ratio (i.e, for a personal care facility in which there is one Days RN per 40 clients, the ratio is 1:40, which gives that facility a rating of 5). Alternatively, the director of care may calculate the number of clients and the staff hours. If you have only one unit, the ratios still work.

SAMPLE

STAFF	INTERMEDIATE CARE 3	RATING
Days RN	FTE 1.5/30	5
Evenings RN	1:30	3
Nights RN	1:40	4
Days RCA	FTE 25/30	4
Evenings RCA	1:10	4
Nights RCA	1:15	4

Staff ratios are determined by the number of clients divided by the number of hours of each category of staff. A regular shift is 7.5 hours. Use the first column of each table to enter the rating calculation if the ratios are not known and hours of staff time are divided into the total number of clients to find the ratio.

Note: FTE stands for Full-Time Equivalent.

Staff Ratios for Personal Care Facilities

Staff	Ratios & Ratings				
Days RN	5 = 1:40	4 = 1:50	3 = 1:60	2 = 1:65	1 = 1:70
Evenings RN	5 = 1:40	4 = 1:50	3 = 1:60	2 = 1:65	1 = 1:70
Nights RN	5 = 1:40	4 = 1:50	3 = 1:60	2 = 1:65	1 = 1:70
Days RCA	5 = 1:15	4 = 1:18	3 = 1:20	2 = 1:25	1 = 1:30
Evenings RCA	5 = 1:15	4 = 1:18	3 = 1:20	2 = 1:25	1 = 1:30
Nights RCA	5 = 1:20	4 = 1:25	3 = 1:30	2 = 1:35	1 = 1:40
Activity Worker	5 = 1:30	4 = 1:40	3 = 1:50	2 = 1:55	1 = 1:60
Administrator	5 = 1:30	4 = 1:40	3 = 1:50	2 = 1:60	1 = 1:65
Cook	5 = 1:100	4 = 1:120	3 = 1:150	2 = 1:175	1 = 1:200
Dental Hygienist	5 = 1:300	4 = 1:350	3 = 1:375	2 = 1:400	1 = 1:500
SUBTOTAL					

Staff	Ratios & Ratings						
Dietary Aides	5 = 1:30	4 = 1:35	3 = 1:45	2 = 1:50	1 = 1:60		
Dietitian	5 = 1:150	4 = 1:175	3 = 1:200	2 = 1:250	1 = 1:275		
Foot Care Nurse	5 = 1:300	4 = 1:350	3 = 1:375	2 = 1:400	1 = 1:500		
Hairdresser	5 = 1:50	4 = 1:60	3 = 1:70	2 = 1:80	1 = 1:90		
Housekeeper	5 = 1:50	4 = 1:60	3 = 1:70	2 = 1:80	1 = 1:90		
Massage	5 = 1:300	4 = 1:350	3 = 1:375	2 = 1:400	1 = 1:500		
Physio/OT	5 = 1:60	4 = 1:70	3 = 1:80	2 = 1:90	1 = 1:100		
Social Worker	5 = 1:60	4 = 1:70	3 = 1:80	2 = 1:90	1 = 1:100		
SUBTOTAL							
TOTAL							

Score ranges for personal care facilities

Questionnaire 1:
Choosing a nursing home _____

Questionnaire 2:
Rating the care _____

Questionnaire 3:
Staff ratios _____

Grand Total _____

To see how the facility rates, compare your grand total to the ratings below. The higher the grand total, the more positive the rating.

5★ = 425–476
4★ = 375–424
3★ = 325–374
2★ = 275–324
1★ = 225–274

Score ranges for intermediate care 2 facilities

Questionnaire 1:
   Choosing a nursing home   _____

Questionnaire 2:
   Rating the care   _____

Questionnaire 3:
   Staff ratios   _____

Grand Total   _____

To see how the facility rates, compare your grand total to the ratings below. The higher the grand total, the more positive the rating.

   5★ = 650–732
   4★ = 600–649
   3★ = 550–599
   2★ = 500–549
   1★ = 450–499

Staff Ratios for Intermediate Care 2 Facilities

Ratios & Ratings

Staff						
Days RN	5 = 1:30	4 = 1:40	3 = 1:50	2 = 1:55	1 = 1:60	
Evenings RN	5 = 1:30	4 = 1:40	3 = 1:50	2 = 1:55	1 = 1:60	
Night RN	5 = 1:30	4 = 1:40	3 = 1:50	2 = 1:55	1 = 1:60	
Days RCA	5 = 1:10	4 = 1:12	3 = 1:15	2 = 1:18	1 = 1:20	
Evenings RCA	5 = 1:12	4 = 1:15	3 = 1:18	2 = 1:20	1 = 1:24	
Nights RCA	5 = 1:20	4 = 1:25	3 = 1:30	2 = 1:35	1 = 1:40	
Activity Worker	5 = 1:30	4 = 1:40	3 = 1:50	2 = 1:55	1 = 1:60	
Administration	5 = 1:30	4 = 1:40	3 = 1:50	2 = 1:55	1 = 1:60	
Art Therapist	5 = 1:200	4 = 1:250	3 = 1:300	2 = 1:350	1 = 1:400	
SUBTOTAL						

Staff	Ratios & Ratings								
Chaplain	5 = 1:250	4 = 1:300	3 = 1:350	2 = 1:400	1 = 1:500				
Clinical Nurse Spec.	5 = 1:200	4 = 1:250	3 = 1:300	2 = 1:350	1 = 1:400				
Cook	5 = 1:100	4 = 1:120	3 = 1:150	2 = 1:175	1 = 1:200				
Dental Hygienist	5 = 1:300	4 = 1:350	3 = 1:375	2 = 1:400	1 = 1:500				
Dietary Aides	5 = 1:25	4 = 1:30	3 = 1:35	2 = 1:40	1 = 1:50				
Dietician	5 = 1:150	4 = 1:175	3 = 1:200	2 = 1:250	1 = 1:300				
Foot Care Nurse	5 = 1:300	4 = 1:350	3 = 1:375	2 = 1:400	1 = 1:500				
Geriatrician	5 = 1:250	4 = 1:300	3 = 1:350	2 = 1:400	1 = 1:500				
Hairdresser	5 = 1:50	4 = 1:60	3 = 1:70	2 = 1:80	1 = 1:90				
SUBTOTAL									

Staff	Ratios & Ratings				
House Physician	5 = 1:20	4 = 1:25	3 = 1:30	2 = 1:35	1 = 1:40
Housekeeper	5 = 1:40	4 = 1:50	3 = 1:60	2 = 1:65	1 = 1:75
Massage	5 = 1:300	4 = 1:350	3 = 1:375	2 = 1:400	1 = 1:500
Music Therapist	5 = 1:150	4 = 1:175	3 = 1:200	2 = 1:250	1 = 1:300
Palliative Care Team	5 = 1:500	4 = 1:600	3 = 1:700	2 = 1:800	1 = 1:900
Pharmacist	5 = 1:80	4 = 1:90	3 = 1:100	2 = 1:120	1 = 1:140
Physio/OT	5 = 1:60	4 = 1:70	3 = 1:80	2 = 1:90	1 = 1:100
Psychogeriatrician	5 = 1:300	4 = 1:350	3 = 1:375	2 = 1:400	1 = 1:500
Psychologist	5 = 1:300	4 = 1:350	3 = 1:375	2 = 1:400	1 = 1:500
SUBTOTAL					

Staff	Ratios & Ratings				
Resp. Therapist IV	5 = 1:500	4 = 1:600	3 = 1:700	4 = 1:800	1 = 1:900
Social Worker	5 = 1:60	4 = 1:70	3 = 1:80	4 = 1:90	1 = 1:100
Speech Language Therapist	5 = 1:150	4 = 1:175	3 = 1:200	4 = 1:250	1 = 1:300
Therapist	5 = 1:500	4 = 1:600	3 = 1:700	4 = 1:800	1 = 1:900
Unit Clerk	5 = 1:80	4 = 1:90	3 = 1:100	4 = 1:120	1 = 1:140
SUBTOTAL					
TOTAL					

Score ranges for intermediate care 3 facilities

Questionnaire 1:
Choosing a nursing home   _____

Questionnaire 2:
Rating the care   _____

Questionnaire 3:
Staff ratios   _____

Grand Total   _____

To see how the facility rates, compare your grand total to the ratings below. The higher the grand total, the more positive the rating.

5★ = 650–732
4★ = 600–649
3★ = 550–599
2★ = 500–549
1★ = 450–499

Score ranges for extended care units or facilities

Questionnaire 1:
  Choosing a nursing home _____

Questionnaire 2:
  Rating the care _____

Questionnaire 3:
  Staff ratios _____

Grand Total _____

To see how the facility rates, compare your grand total to the ratings below. The higher the grand total, the more positive the rating.

  5* = 650–732
  4* = 600–649
  3* = 550–599
  2* = 500–549
  1* = 450–499

Staff Ratios for Intermediate Care 3 Facilities

Staff	Ratios & Ratings					
Days RN	5 = 1:20	4 = 1:25	3 = 1:30	2 = 1:35	1 = 1:40	
Evenings RN	5 = 1:20	4 = 1:25	3 = 1:30	2 = 1:35	1 = 1:40	
Night RN	5 = 1:30	4 = 1:40	3 = 1:50	2 = 1:55	1 = 1:60	
Days RCA	5 = 1:8	4 = 1:10	3 = 1:12	2 = 1:14	1 = 1:16	
Evenings RCA	5 = 1:10	4 = 1:12	3 = 1:15	2 = 1:18	1 = 1:20	
Nights RCA	5 = 1:12	4 = 1:15	3 = 1:18	2 = 1:20	1 = 1:24	
Activity Worker	5 = 1:30	4 = 1:40	3 = 1:50	2 = 1:55	1 = 1:60	
Administration	5 = 1:30	4 = 1:40	3 = 1:50	2 = 1:55	1 = 1:60	
Art Therapist	5 = 1:200	4 = 1:250	3 = 1:300	2 = 1:350	1 = 1:400	
SUBTOTAL						

Staff	Ratios & Ratings				
Chaplain	5 = 1:250	4 = 1:300	3 = 1:350	2 = 1:400	1 = 1:500
Clinical Nurse Spec.	5 = 1:200	4 = 1:250	3 = 1:300	2 = 1:350	1 = 1:400
Cook	5 = 1:100	4 = 1:120	3 = 1:150	2 = 1:175	1 = 1:200
Dental Hygienist	5 = 1:300	4 = 1:350	3 = 1:375	2 = 1:400	1 = 1:500
Dietary Aides	5 = 1:25	4 = 1:30	3 = 1:35	2 = 1:40	1 = 1:50
Dietician	5 = 1:150	4 = 1:175	3 = 1:200	2 = 1:250	1 = 1:300
Foot Care Nurse	5 = 1:300	4 = 1:350	3 = 1:375	2 = 1:400	1 = 1:500
Geriatrician	5 = 1:250	4 = 1:300	3 = 1:350	2 = 1:400	1 = 1:500
Hairdresser	5 = 1:50	4 = 1:60	3 = 1:70	2 = 1:80	1 = 1:90
SUBTOTAL					

Staff	Ratios & Ratings				
House Physician	5 = 1:20	4 = 1:25	3 = 1:30	2 = 1:35	1 = 1:40
Housekeeper	5 = 1:40	4 = 1:50	3 = 1:60	2 = 1:65	1 = 1:75
Massage	5 = 1:300	4 = 1:350	3 = 1:375	2 = 1:400	1 = 1:500
Music Therapist	5 = 1:150	4 = 1:175	3 = 1:200	2 = 1:250	1 = 1:300
Palliative Care Team	5 = 1:500	4 = 1:600	3 = 1:700	2 = 1:800	1 = 1:900
Pharmacist	5 = 1:80	4 = 1:90	3 = 1:100	2 = 1:120	1 = 1:140
Physio/OT	5 = 1:60	4 = 1:70	3 = 1:80	2 = 1:90	1 = 1:100
Psychogeriatrician	5 = 1:300	4 = 1:350	3 = 1:375	2 = 1:400	1 = 1:500
Psychologist	5 = 1:300	4 = 1:350	3 = 1:375	2 = 1:400	1 = 1:500
SUBTOTAL					

Staff	Ratios & Ratings				
Resp. Therapist IV	5 = 1:500	4 = 1:600	3 = 1:700	4 = 1:800	1 = 1:900
Social Worker	5 = 1:60	4 = 1:70	3 = 1:80	4 = 1:90	1 = 1:100
Speech Language Therapist	5 = 1:150	4 = 1:175	3 = 1:200	4 = 1:250	1 = 1:300
Therapist	5 = 1:500	4 = 1:600	3 = 1:700	4 = 1:800	1 = 1:900
Unit Clerk	5 = 1:80	4 = 1:90	3 = 1:100	4 = 1:120	1 = 1:140
SUBTOTAL					
TOTAL					

Staff Ratios for Extended Care Units or Facilities

Staff   Ratios & Ratings

Staff					
Days RN	5 = 1:15	4 = 1:18	3 = 1:20	2 = 1:25	1 = 1:30
Evenings RN	5 = 1:25	4 = 1:30	3 = 1:35	2 = 1:40	1 = 1:50
Night RN	5 = 1:30	4 = 1:40	3 = 1:50	2 = 1:55	1 = 1:60
Days RCA	5 = 1:5	4 = 1:7	3 = 1:9	2 = 1:11	1 = 1:13
Evenings RCA	5 = 1:7	4 = 1:9	3 = 1:11	2 = 1:13	1 = 1:15
Nights RCA	5 = 1:10	4 = 1:12	3 = 1:14	2 = 1:16	1 = 1:20
Activity Worker	5 = 1:30	4 = 1:40	3 = 1:50	2 = 1:55	1 = 1:60
Administration	5 = 1:30	4 = 1:40	3 = 1:50	2 = 1:55	1 = 1:60
Art Therapist	5 = 1:200	4 = 1:250	3 = 1:300	2 = 1:350	1 = 1:400
SUBTOTAL					

Staff	Ratios & Ratings				
Chaplain	5 = 1:250	4 = 1:300	3 = 1:350	2 = 1:400	1 = 1:500
Clinical Nurse Spec.	5 = 1:200	4 = 1:250	3 = 1:300	2 = 1:350	1 = 1:400
Cook	5 = 1:100	4 = 1:120	3 = 1:150	2 = 1:175	1 = 1:200
Dental Hygienist	5 = 1:300	4 = 1:350	3 = 1:375	2 = 1:400	1 = 1:500
Dietary Aides	5 = 1:25	4 = 1:30	3 = 1:35	2 = 1:40	1 = 1:50
Dietician	5 = 1:150	4 = 1:175	3 = 1:200	2 = 1:250	1 = 1:300
Foot Care Nurse	5 = 1:300	4 = 1:350	3 = 1:375	2 = 1:400	1 = 1:500
Geriatrician	5 = 1:250	4 = 1:300	3 = 1:350	2 = 1:400	1 = 1:500
Hairdresser	5 = 1:50	4 = 1:60	3 = 1:70	2 = 1:80	1 = 1:90
SUBTOTAL					

Staff	Ratios & Ratings				
House Physician	5 = 1:20	4 = 1:25	3 = 1:30	2 = 1:35	1 = 1:40
Housekeeper	5 = 1:40	4 = 1:50	3 = 1:60	2 = 1:65	1 = 1:75
Massage	5 = 1:300	4 = 1:350	3 = 1:375	2 = 1:400	1 = 1:500
Music Therapist	5 = 1:150	4 = 1:175	3 = 1:200	2 = 1:250	1 = 1:275
Palliative Care Team	5 = 1:500	4 = 1:600	3 = 1:700	2 = 1:800	1 = 1:900
Pharmacist	5 = 1:80	4 = 1:90	3 = 1:100	2 = 1:120	1 = 1:140
Physio/OT	5 = 1:60	4 = 1:70	3 = 1:80	2 = 1:90	1 = 1:100
Psychogeriatrician	5 = 1:300	4 = 1:350	3 = 1:375	2 = 1:400	1 = 1:500
Psychologist	5 = 1:300	4 = 1:350	3 = 1:375	2 = 1:400	1 = 1:500
SUBTOTAL					

Staff	Ratios & Ratings				
Resp. Therapist IV	5 = 1:500	4 = 1:600	3 = 1:700	4 = 1:800	1 = 1:900
Social Worker	5 = 1:60	4 = 1:70	3 = 1:80	4 = 1:90	1 = 1:100
Speech Language Therapist	5 = 1:150	4 = 1:175	3 = 1:200	4 = 1:250	1 = 1:300
Therapist	5 = 1:500	4 = 1:600	3 = 1:700	4 = 1:800	1 = 1:900
Unit Clerk	5 = 1:80	4 = 1:90	3 = 1:100	4 = 1:120	1 = 1:140
SUBTOTAL					
TOTAL					

Chapter 10

HOW TO BE ADMITTED TO A NURSING HOME

You've known for a while that you cannot continue living on your own without some help. You've spoken with your family and friends, considered what level of care you need, and looked into the various housing options available in your community. Part 1 of this book has helped you do this.

Once you determined the best housing option for yourself, you evaluated the nursing homes on your list using the questionnaires in Part 2 of this book. You've made your decision, and now it's time to apply to the care facility you have chosen.

This chapter leads you through the process of being admitted to a government-supported nursing home. Because you are paying out of your own pocket for your care in a private nursing home, the admission procedure for private homes is often less bureaucratic than for a government-

291

supported home and there aren't usually long wait lists.

One thing to remember when you move into a government-supported facility is that you may lose some of your state or provincial medical benefits. This may mean that if your physician prescribes drugs that are not on the formulary list, you have to pay for alternate, new, or experimental drugs. This is a distinct disadvantage to poorer clients.

Determining Eligibility

In the United States, as part of admission to a nursing home, a client must be evaluated on the federal standardized assessment, called the Minimum Data Set (MDS). The MDS provides a comprehensive screening and assessment for all clients of Medicare and Medicaid long-term care facilities and helps standardize how health care professionals communicate about client problems and facilities. The MDS looks at the client's physical, emotional, mental, cognitive, and functional limitations and strengths. All Medicare and Medicaid clients must be assessed at the time of admission, quarterly, annually, and when a significant change in their condition occurs. In addition, the client's insurer may provide funds and specify for which nursing homes the client is eligible.

In Canada, in order to be admitted to a government-supported nursing home, you must be referred or refer yourself to the continuing care division of your regional health board. Physicians and other health professionals will perform an assessment of your health-care needs. They will look at factors such as your medical history, prescriptions, treatments, and prognosis. An assessor (nurse or social worker) from the continuing care division of the health unit will evaluate your ability to perform tasks (e.g., activities of daily living such as bathing yourself and instrumental activities of daily living such as food preparation). This is usually done by asking questions. Your mental ability is also assessed by asking a group of specific questions such as, "Who is the current prime minister of Canada?"

Before you can be considered for admission to a long-term care facility in Canada, you must be eligible for long-term care program benefits (i.e., you must meet the residency requirements and have pension benefits in place). All appropriate home support services must have thoroughly been tried and found to be inadequate to meet your needs. Usually, you can only get care in a facility when home support services do not meet your individual needs. For this reason, home support services are normally provided for a trial period before residential care is approved.

Chapter 3 outlines the categories used to assess your health care needs.

Getting on the Wait List

If you qualify, you are given a choice of facilities within your area that meet your specific care requirements. You are required to view the facilities of your choice before you will be put on the wait list. Phone the contact person to make an appointment. Take with you the questionnaires included in this book when you view the facilities so that you can evaluate them and choose the best home for your needs and those of your family.

After viewing and deciding to which facility you want to be admitted, contact your long-term care case manager, who will place your name on the wait list. You and/or your family must agree to pay the daily rate plus the room differential, if applicable.

Most government-supported facilities have wait lists. When the wait list is long, and admission unlikely to take place for some time, you may decide to choose a facility with a shorter list as an alternative or another form of supportive housing. In reality, however, little choice exists because other supportive housing is not readily available in many communities.

Being Admitted

Only clients prepared to accept immediate placement are placed on the waiting list. For government-supported facilities, a client has 48 hours to move when a bed becomes available. If the client refuses the bed, he or she goes to the bottom of the list.

Emergency admissions are restricted to clients whose necessary care can no longer be provided at home because of unacceptable risk to client, caregiver, or community.

If your care needs change in the future, unless you are in a multilevel care facility, you may have to move to a different facility.

In Canada, because of a shortage of facilities, elders are often encouraged to take the first available bed and are told they can transfer to another facility that better suits their needs at a later date.

This seldom works out successfully for the elder because the move into the first nursing home is so traumatic that a second move becomes a major hurdle.

The US health care system is more conducive to movement between facilities because it is governed by free enterprise. You enter a nursing home to recuperate and you leave as soon as possible to save money. There is more competition to attract residents, so more services and amenities are available. Insurance companies and health maintenance organizations have programs such as day care and home care to prevent elders from having to enter a nursing home.

Making the Move

Whether your new home will be a private facility or a government-supported one, making the move can be traumatic for you and your family. Your old residence needs to be cleaned out and may need to be sold.

You will have to choose which possessions to take with you. Usually you have a lot less space available to you in a nursing home than you are used to. If you are moving into a one- or two-room facility, you may consider taking a dresser, bedside table, small bookshelf, and easy chair. You will need to consider which clothes to pack because wardrobe space may be limited. Don't forget also to include some personal belongings such as paintings or photographs to make the room feel like home.

Settling In

Studies show that admission to a nursing home is so stressful that some clients die within the first three months. Because moving is difficult for most elders, good nursing homes have an in-depth orientation to make that move easier. Both the client and his or her family should be able to attend it. The orientation team should include members of staff as well as other clients and even family members. During the orientation, the client will be introduced to key personnel and shown the physical environment of the facility (i.e., where the dining room is, where the social activities are held, how to get hold of a resident care aide in an emergency). If the client is sharing a room with other clients, he or she will also be introduced to his or her roommates. The client should receive an orientation booklet outlining all the facilities available in the home.

In an ideal situation, a nursing home provides support to clients with the purpose of enhancing their independence. However, in most cases, fostering and encouraging independence is not a reality. Often clients become dependent because the staff does everything for them. They lose their sense of control and become institutionalized. However, with some effort on the part of the client and his or her family, admission to a nursing home can improve the client's quality of life. Having trained professionals to look after the client can allow him or her to enjoy social activities or pursue other interests. If the client takes part in the activities arranged by the home, he or she will get the most out of his or her stay there.

Chapter 11

LEGAL MATTERS AND DECISIONS

There are many things you need to consider when deciding on your future housing options. Apart from deciding what kind of care you need and can afford and where you can best find that care in your community, you also need to consider certain legal questions. For example, if you are incapacitated, whom do you want to make decisions for you? If you fall ill, what level of medical intervention do you want?

Although these decisions about life and health care are all reversible as circumstances change, it is a good idea to think about your choices now and spell them out as precisely as possible. By appointing someone you know and trust to make decisions in your place, you are protected against having a stranger make decisions for you. The best time to think about these issues is long before you get ill.

A discussion of these issues would be

more complex than the scope of this book allows, but this chapter briefly outlines some legal considerations that apply to elders — whether or not you are in a nursing home. For more detailed information, please consult one of the following books in the Self-Counsel Press series:

* *Wills Guide for America*
* *Wills Guide for Canada*
* *Your Health-Care Directive*
* *Power of Attorney Kit*

Who Will Make Decisions for You If You Become Incapacitated?

If you become incapacitated, someone else will have to take over decisions related to your health, personal, and physical care. Someone will also have to make decisions about your finances and property.

According to the law in most states and provinces, if you do not appoint someone to make these decisions for you, the courts will do so for you. This means that a member of your family or the Public Guardian and Trustee will have power over your health, personal, and physical care, as well as over your property and financial matters. Unless you have discussed your wishes with your family and

300

these people, you will have no say in what happens to you.

If you're like most of us, you would prefer to have someone you know and trust look after your affairs should you become incapacitated in the future. Before entering a nursing home, you may wish to consult a lawyer to draw up either or both of the following documents:

* Durable/enduring power of attorney
* Advance directive/representation agreement

Sometimes you can combine these two documents into one all-purpose guardianship document. Your lawyer will be able to advise you on the laws in your state or province and can prepare the necessary documents.

Power of Attorney

When you give someone the power of attorney over your finances and property, it means that you have authorized them to act as a substitute decision-maker (i.e., they can make decisions on your behalf in matters affecting these areas of your life if you are unable to do so yourself). You should talk to your lawyer before you sign any kind of power of attorney. In some states and provinces, the power you grant to your representative can be used immediately, whether or not you are incapacitated.

Choose your substitute decision-maker well. That person may be making decisions about your finances and property that could affect the quality of health care you receive in the future.

Advance Directives for Health Care

Advance health care directives allow you to state your wishes about certain kinds of health care decisions or medical procedures. Depending on where you live, these documents may also be called living wills, personal directives, health care powers of attorney, or representation agreements.

A health care directive allows your substitute decision-maker to tell the doctor what type of health care you want to receive if you are unable to make the decision yourself. For example, he or she may sign the permission or authorization for your flu shots to protect you against pneumonia.

A living will says how you feel about medical care that will artificially prolong your life. It can instruct your medical care providers and family to withdraw artificial support at a certain point, although it can also be used to say that you actually want your life prolonged by artificial means.

A living will can also contain do not resuscitate (DNR) orders. These include:

* *Level 1:* You want comfort measures only, food and water by mouth. Staff can position you to keep you comfortable but they give you no medication. You have made the choice to die without any medical interference.

* *Level 2:* You want comfort measures and oral medication (e.g., antibiotics) to keep you alive.

* *Level 3:* You want physicians to order invasive procedures to keep you alive (e.g., an intravenous or a nasogastric tube put down your nose so they can feed you).

* *Level 4:* You want all the above interventions plus cardiac pulmonary resuscitation (CPR) in the event of cardiac arrest (i.e., you want medical staff to breathe into your mouth, pump your chest manually, and with electrical shock revive you and start your heart pumping blood again). You are being kept alive on a respirator.

Make sure you discuss your resuscitation wishes with your physician prior to admission to a nursing home. You need to be very clear and explain what level of medical intervention is acceptable to you.

The laws around advance directives for health care differ widely across the United States and Canada. Your lawyer will be able to advise you about your situation. Remember, too, to discuss your wishes with your family and substitute decision-maker. He or she must be aware of what you want and must also be comfortable making these kinds of decisions for you. Make sure the staff of your nursing home and your personal physician know what your advance directive says to avoid confusion later on.

Wills

To ensure that your assets are distributed the way you want them to be when you die, you need to write a will. Without a will, state or provincial laws determine how your property will be distributed to your survivors. These laws may not reflect your wishes regarding who should get your property after you die. Review your will yearly and update it whenever a major event happens in your life, such as marriage, divorce, the birth of children, or the deaths of loved ones.

Proper estate planning will allow you to manage your money and property during your lifetime to create a comfortable life and retirement for yourself, while also providing for those you love after your death. Good estate planning includes assistance from many different professional advisors, such as your lawyer, banker, accountant, and insurance agent.

Chapter 12

MAKING COMPLAINTS AND DEALING WITH ABUSE

Case Study

A Complaint Gone out of Control:
Mr. Thomas's Story

Mr. Thomas's wife, Mrs. Thomas, lived in a nursing home close to where he lived. Mr. Thomas went to see his wife every day and did what he could to keep her calm and happy. Before her admission, he had looked after her at home, and he knew what a difficult task it was to take care of her. As her dementia progressed, she took to wandering the streets and became incontinent and combative. His worry and fatigue from caring for her led to clinical anxiety depression, for which he was treated by a psychiatrist just before and after her admission. Although he was happier now and feeling less guilty about being unable to help her at home, he still worried about her.

One day, the nursing home called Mr. Thomas and his daughter, Susan, to a special family conference about his wife. The clinical nurse specialist and social worker who set up the meeting wanted to discuss with the director of care and family some of the problems the resident care aides were having with Mrs. Thomas. She had dementia and was becoming very difficult to transfer into a chair because she resisted and complained to the staff. She was also unhappy about a lot of things, including the food.

Mr. Thomas had previously mentioned his concerns about the care of his wife to the director of care, but she had just written in the chart that this man complained about everything and was overprotective. The director of care, who chaired and controlled the conference, wanted to find solutions to make the life of her staff easier, and glossed over Mr. Thomas's complaint. Instead of feeling comfortable to speak up at the meeting, Mr. Thomas felt intimidated by all the professionals sitting around discussing his wife in scientific terms. The only thing he really understood was what the dietician had to say (because Mrs. Thomas liked ice cream and hated milk, the staff decided to give her ice cream at every meal). The problem with Mrs. Thomas not liking the staff was mentioned but not resolved.

A week after the special family conference, while visiting his wife, Mr. Thomas saw a resident care aide push his wife roughly into the chair. Mr. Thomas lodged a complaint with the clinical nurse specialist, who took him to see the manager of the facility. The manager assured Mr. Thomas that something would be done about it. During the next two days, nothing changed, and the same resident care aide still looked after his wife. He spoke to the director of care, who questioned whether he had really seen the abuse. He emphatically stated his case again and reminded her that he had already reported the incident to her when it happened.

Mr. Thomas felt that the manager and director of care did not believe his story and he could not find the clinical nurse specialist. (She was on holidays.) He remembered that the social worker had been kind to him at the family conference, so he told her about the abuse and explained how upset he was.

Three weeks went by, and still nothing happened. Mr. Thomas was very upset that the same resident care aide was still looking after his wife. He told his daughter, and they phoned the Alzheimer's Society, which referred them to a lawyer. The lawyer started to investigate the incident. Because the manager was now on holidays along with the clinical nurse specialist, the lawyer talked to the vice-president of the facility. The vice-president had not been aware of the incident, so she investigated.

She found that an e-mail had been sent to the manager from the clinical nurse specialist about the incident. The manager had interviewed everyone separately. The director of care had told her Mr. Thomas was a busybody who was just causing trouble and had written in the chart that he was seeing things that were not there, suggesting he might need psychiatric evaluation. The manager had asked a psychiatrist to examine Mr. Thomas to see if he was going into clinical depression again. She had not told Mr. Thomas she was doing this, so he was confused by the strange man who had visited him and asked all sorts of questions. The resident care aide said that nothing had happened. The manager chose to believe the resident care aide and let the case drop. She did not talk to

Mr. Thomas again or tell him about her decision not to make any change in staffing.

The vice-president was horrified at the charting and lack of follow-up done by the manager. It would have been so easy to suspend the resident care aide with pay until she had investigated and communicated the results to Mr. Thomas with his daughter and social worker present. Her lack of action put the facility at risk of being sued. The union was strongly behind the resident care aide, and both the manager's job as well the director of care's (to whom the resident care aide reported) were now in jeopardy. If the manager had addressed the issue at the beginning, the others (the clinical nurse specialist, social worker, manager, and vice-president) would not have been involved.

To allay the situation, the vice-president offered to move Mrs. Thomas to another facility or to another floor. Both options were unacceptable because Mr. Thomas just wanted his wife to stay where she was. He regretted complaining because he now felt all the staff were against him and were defensive, and his wife was suffering from lack of care.

The legal battle was long and involved. In court, the resident care aide testified that it was difficult to transfer Mrs. Thomas to the chair, and that she had not used the proper body mechanics to do so. When Mrs. Thomas squirmed in her arms, the resident care aide lost her balance and pushed her into the chair to save both of them from falling. This was the pushing that Mr. Thomas had seen, but according to the resident care aide, it was unintentional. She went on to say that she had lied and denied the incident because she knew she was wrong not to have called for help to move Mrs. Thomas, and was at fault for using poor body mechanics. She did not want to get into trouble. The director of care had believed the resident care aide. By writing in the chart about the need for a psychiatrist to examine Mr. Thomas, she had over-stepped the bounds of her authority and trodden on his rights.

Mr. Thomas won the case, but it generated much bad publicity for the facility. The director of care and manager were both removed from their positions. His wife remained in the unit while the resident care aide was removed to another unit. The money from the legal case was used to hire private resident care aides that Mr. and Mrs. Thomas both liked.

The story of Mr. Thomas's complaints is a sad one. Because the facility was at fault and mismanaged the complaint, it grew out of proportion unnecessarily. Mr. Thomas had a right to complain based on what he saw (whether or not the resident care aide's actions were intentional). He told the correct person, the director of care, who was in a position to solve the problem. That was the first break in the chain. The second break was the fact that the case was not pursued, because the clinical nurse specialist and then the manager went on holidays, and so the problem was neither resolved nor sufficiently investigated. The facility claimed to be client-centered, but the solutions the vice-president gave to Mr. Thomas were anything but that. Moving Mrs. Thomas to a new floor would not have been in her best interests. The best solution was for the resident care aide to be removed, and that happened only when their backs were to the wall. An ombudsman appointed by the nursing home would have solved this complaint without the need for a lengthy court battle.

Mrs. Thomas was lucky to have had someone to fight for her rights. Many other stories of abuse go unreported and unresolved. This chapter deals with some of the different types of abuse elders may face in a nursing home, and provides strategies for making complaints that will be dealt with effectively.

How to Complain in a Nursing Home

Complaints are common in nursing homes and are usually valid. Although facilities claim they are client-centered and give individualized special consideration and care to all clients, they are, after all, institutions. Because of the number of people under one roof, not every client can have his or her own schedule accommodated; otherwise, chaos would result. But by working together in a nonconfrontational way, staff, family, and clients can usually find a workable solution for specific problems.

Handling complaints in a nursing home can be a time-consuming business and takes considerable negotiating skill and knowledge and much creative thinking. It is often best for a facility to have a designated ombudsman, that is, someone who is not directly involved in client care but who is approachable, friendly, and knowledgeable about the running of the facility. This person may handle complaints not only from clients and relatives but also from staff.

Chain of command is hierarchical in most facilities. It is best to first try to deal with a complaint at the direct care-giving level before escalating to a higher level. If you are unhappy about something, follow the chain of command set out below. (Note that your facility may have all or only some of the staff listed.)

1. First, consult the resident care aide or certified nurse assistant who directly looks after you or your loved one.

2. If this is not practical or you do not feel comfortable speaking to this person, then seek out the charge nurse, licensed practical nurse, or registered nurse in charge of that particular unit. Some facilities may also have a nurse manager.

3. If he or she does not take satisfactory action, then proceed to the director of care or long-term care director, and

finally to the administrator or chief executive officer.

4. In private personal care and intermediate care level 1 facilities, and some extended care facilities, the owner is your last resort. If a charitable group administers the home, see a member of the board of directors or, ultimately, the chairperson of the board.

5. If all else fails in a privately run institution, you may complain to the health board in your region, because the facility is licensed. Find the person responsible for licensing that particular facility, and then the chief operating officer for regional health geriatric services in nursing homes.

6. The chief operating officer reports to provincial or state government people. Therefore, as a last resort you can try to resolve your complaint at that level by contacting the state or provincial elected person responsible for geriatric services in nursing homes. You can also contact your state ombudsman or member of congress. Long before you reach this point, you ought to have resolved your problem.

7. In the US, the state department of social and health services (or some similar title) is responsible for licensing and regulatory controls. They can be contacted directly or anonymously.

The purpose of outlining the above procedure for complaints is to give you some insight into the avenues open to you. Complaints ought to be resolved at a local level. Only cases of severe mismanagement get out of hand, and in such cases, an ombudsman can often help the client and his or her family avoid the stress of a legal struggle — as well as save the facility many thousands of dollars in legal fees and a great deal of bad publicity.

Dealing with Elder Abuse

Elder abuse is defined as "any action by someone in a position of trust that causes harm to an older person." Types of elder abuse can include physical, financial or economic, psychological or emotional, sexual, medication, or violation of civil/ human rights, and there may be varying levels of abuse within these categories.

Nursing home staff can sometimes abuse clients because they are in a position of power over them. Just by their position alone, they must be careful not to intimidate or abuse clients. Nonetheless, clients can be very aggressive with staff. They can fight them physically, bite, scratch, kick, and generally physically abuse them. Clients can also emotionally abuse staff by making slighting remarks and ethnic slurs. However, staff as professionals need to discuss and implement procedures to eliminate abuse of any kind.

Abuse is common and unrecognized by many elders and their relatives. It is not mandatory to report the abuse of elders (as it is when children are involved), and there is very little public awareness about the nature of elder abuse. Many elders who are abused have no one to advocate for them, and many cases of abuse go unreported. There must be zero tolerance for any kind of abuse.

Complaints of abuse are not very common, probably because many people are not aware of what constitutes abuse. Most people are afraid to complain because they fear their loved one will be mistreated. That is only natural, and that is why an officially appointed ombudsman in a nursing home fulfills such an important role. Mistakes made need to be addressed and rectified because most staff are very devoted, caring people.

Physical abuse

Physical abuse includes beating, throwing a person down, using a weapon against a person, twisting arms, tripping, biting, pushing, shoving, hitting, slapping, choking, pulling hair, punching, kicking, or grabbing. Physical abuse also includes deliberate exposure to severe weather and unnecessary physical restraint. (See later in this chapter for more on restraints.) Physical abuse of elders is the ultimate offence and is punishable by law.

Financial abuse

Financial abuse is misuse of an elder's funds or property through fraud, trickery, or force. Financial abuse also includes cashing of pension checks, overcharging for room and board or for small services, trying to make an elder give up something of value, or attempting to persuade him or her to sign over the house. Financial abuse is also punishable by law.

According to Canadian studies, financial abuse is the most common type of elder abuse, usually by distant relatives, friends, or neighbors rather than close relatives.

The study further found that the typical elder who is financially abused is a single person with health problems and who is somewhat isolated.

Psychological and emotional abuse

Psychological abuse includes verbal aggression, humiliation, isolation, intimidation, threats, and inappropriate control of activities. It also includes removal of decision-making power while someone is still competent, withholding affection for manipulative purposes, refusing access to grandchildren, and denying privacy in facilities.

Nursing homes need to be very aware that they could be perceived as potential abusers to their frail clients because they have the capacity to isolate them. They can control what a client does, whom he or she sees and talks to and where he or she goes. Because the resident care aides give intimate direct care to clients in nursing homes, they need to be aware of providing privacy, especially when they expose a client for care or a diaper change. Resident care aides can intimidate clients and make them fearful just by looks, actions, gestures, talking in a loud voice, smashing things, or destroying property.

If nursing home staff make all the decisions for clients, it could be considered psychological abuse. Staff need to be sensitive about how they can easily put clients down and make them feel bad. For example, when a client is incontinent, the resident care aide is psychologically abusive if she makes him feel bad about loss of control of his bowel or bladder. Even an "Oh! Not again!" comment is demeaning and a form of abuse. Mind games and making someone think he or she is crazy are both also abuse.

Sexual abuse
Unwanted sexual activity, such as verbal or suggestive behavior, fondling, sexual intercourse, or lack of personal privacy are all forms of sexual abuse. In nursing homes, the most common form is lack of privacy and rough handling when toileting clients. Sexual abuse is also a type of physical abuse.

Nursing homes ought to include sexual needs as part of their client assessment. It is important to provide a room with a closed door, and staff must never enter any room without knocking or asking permission. A gray area exists here for clients with dementia-type symptoms who are declared incompetent. Are they able to consent to sex with other clients? These circumstances present an ethical dilemma that staff and families must resolve individually.

Medication abuse

Medication abuse is the misuse of an elder's medications and prescriptions, including withholding medication, overmedicating an elder, or not complying with prescription refills. Many elders are abused by overmedication to keep them from disrupting the other clients and staff. See the section on use of restraints later in this chapter for more information on medication as a chemical restraint.

Violation of civil and human rights

Violation of civil and human rights is primarily the denial of an elder's fundamental rights according to legislation, the Bill of Rights (US), the Charter of Rights and Freedoms (Canada), and the United Nations Declaration of Human Rights. Examples of violations of rights include withholding information; denying privacy, visitors, or religious worship; restricting liberty; unwarranted confining to a hospital or institution; and interfering with mail.

US federal law has outlined specific rights that offer protection to nursing home residents. Every nursing home client has the right to the following:

* Respect
* Freedom from discrimination
* Freedom from abuse
* Freedom from restraints
* Information on services and fees
* Freedom to manage his or her own money
* Privacy, property, and living arrangements
* Access to medical care by his or her own physician, and to be informed of his or her own illness, and to refuse care
* Visitors' privacy, and visitation at any time
* Social services
* Freedom to leave
* Freedom to complain without fear of punishment
* Protection against unfair transfer or discharge

Case Study

A Story of Abuse: Mr. Helm's Story

As Mr. Helm approached the open front door of the nursing home, he could smell that acrid scent of urine. He was coming to see his wife in her nursing home, as he did every day, but today the smell was worse than he remembered. He entered the front lounge and saw his wife slumped down in her wheelchair sitting with ten other clients all vacantly looking into space. Mrs. Helm had a tray across her chair and a lap belt tied around her middle. Her feet were blue with cold and shod in unmatched shoes. When Mrs. Helm saw her husband, she started to cry. He bent down and kissed her on her forehead because there was food still sticking to the corners of her mouth. It was mid-morning, and Mrs. Helm was sitting in her wet diaper. She had squirmed around so much that the rug over her knees had fallen to the ground and her head was barely above the restraining table in front of her. If she were left like that much longer, she might slither down out of the lap belt restraint and strangle herself on it.

In the lounge, another man, with head

bent, was engrossed in his lap belt and struggling to cut it with nail scissors. Mr. Helm went to find some help. No one was in sight, but he noticed a group of resident care aides talking to each other down a corridor outside the staff coffee room. He politely asked if someone could help him move his wife up in her chair and take her back to her room to change her because she was soaking wet. One exasperated resident care aide called into the coffee room and said, "Ally, she's your patient today. I guess you have to change her again." There was a grumble heard from the back of the coffee room, and slowly a resident care aide emerged to go with Mr. Helm. As they walked the hall, she told Mr. Helm that she was really tired. Her husband had left her a few weeks ago, and she was having trouble finding day care for her sick child, who had kept her up all night.

Mr. Helm felt sorry for this resident care aide and was apologetic that he had to disturb her, but his wife was in distress. The resident care aide approached Mrs. Helm from behind and grabbed her under the armpits from the back of the wheelchair and roughly pulled her to a sitting position. Mrs. Helm was visibly startled and began to scream. The resident care aide said nothing but looked exasperated. She then grudgingly pulled the rug from the floor to push Mrs. Helm to her room because it was in the way of the wheelchair.

The resident care aide told Mr. Helm to leave the room because she was going to change his wife. He did not want to leave because he had been looking after all his wife's needs for the past 50 years. As she had become more demented, he had been the one to change her. However, the resident care aide pushed him gently out of the room and closed the door.

All this time, Mrs. Helm had been crying quietly, but now Mr. Helm could hear her wails increase. She was screaming for help, and then the screaming became muffled. Mr. Helm could not stand it. He opened the door to see his wife on her stomach with her face in the pillow. Her sweatpants had been pulled down around her ankles so she could not kick her feet, and the resident care aide was slapping cream on her angry-red-looking bottom. She growled at him to get out because she would be finished shortly. At that moment, Mr. Helm also saw red chafe marks on her waist from the lap belt.

The resident care aide turned Mrs. Helm over, completely exposing her nakedness, while pulling off the restraining sweatpants and throwing them on the floor beside the bed. The resident care aide then went to the other side of the room to get a diaper. Mrs. Helm was quieter now, but the tears were streaming down her face. With the diaper changed, side rails pulled up, the resident care aide left the room. The dirty sweatpants remained beside the bed.

Meanwhile, back in the common room, a great ruckus was going on. A resident care aide was wrestling with the man with the nail scissors, who was wildly yelling profanities. He was threatening her with them because he would not give them up. The director of care was called, and she sat beside the man and negotiated with him to give up the scissors if the lap belt was removed. This was the second seat belt he had cut in two days. He had fallen a week ago, and although he had suffered nothing more than bruises from the fall, the staff decided he needed to be restrained.

Use of Restraints in Nursing Homes

Restraints are physical, chemical, or environmental measures used to control the physical behavioral activity of a person or portion of his or her body. Physical restraints limit a client's movement. These may include lap belts, a table fixed to a chair, or a raised bed rail that the client cannot lower. Environmental restraints control a client's mobility. These include placing clients in a secure locked unit or garden and a seclusion or time-out room. Chemical restraint refers to any form of psychoactive medication used not to treat an illness but to intentionally inhibit a particular behavior or movement. Chemical restraint could be used to curb wandering or disruptive behavior or to chemically castrate an elder.

Research shows that use of restraints causes more harm than good. Unfortunately, the use of restraints in nursing homes is an all-too-common occurrence. Staff justifies the use of restraints because they think they are protecting clients from injury, maintaining treatment, or controlling disruptive behavior. In fact, falls that occur in a non-restraint setting are proven to cause less harm to the client than when the client is restrained. The current research has shown that the use of restraints is actually associated with increased incidence of injury, skin breakdown, functional decline, loss of appetite, dehydration, constipation, disoriented behavior, and emotional distress. In some cases, clients have died from strangulation as they struggled against the restraint.

Least-Restraint Policy

Least-restraint is a policy directive that means all possible alternative interventions have been exhausted before deciding to use a restraint. All nursing homes must have a least-restraint policy because restraining an individual is against his or her legal rights.

Toileting patterns are a common cause of behaviour that may (unnecessarily) lead to restraint. For example, an unruly client may have peed in his diaper and would thus be uncomfortable and desperate for someone to notice him. A client who has fallen out of her bed could have been wanting to go to the bathroom, but was prevented from doing so because the bed rail was up and she had to climb over the side rail or the end of the bed. In many cases, climbing over side rails results in a severe fall by which many clients break their hips.

If a facility has a least-restraint policy, staff will explore other alternatives before restraining clients. In the above case, staff should have observed the client more carefully in order to recognize patterns and develop a toileting program. A bed alarm could be installed that alerts resident care aides when a client leaves his or her bed and needs help. Or the bed could be moved closer to the floor so that the client can then safely get in and out of bed at will.

Under a least-restraint program, nurses assess and analyze what is causing the relevant behavior before resorting to restraining clients. Usually a pattern of behavior can be determined. Perhaps clients attempt to get up from their chairs or beds because they are bored or are in pain. Restraining them in wheelchairs or with bed rails is not the solution. A supervised program of walking and physical exercise could stop clients from wandering. Clients who fall frequently may have an unsteady gait. A physiotherapist may help assess the cause and come up with a walking program to increase steadiness or strength in leg muscles or improve gait. Sometimes, it is as simple as a new pair of good, supportive shoes (i.e., with Velcro fasteners that are very helpful and easy for clients to put on and take off).

Choices and Risk

Today's health care philosophies advocate the rights of clients to make their own decisions regarding care. Health care professionals recognize that elders must have the choice to accept the risk of harm, as long as they understand the nature of the risk. This means that nurses may respect client wishes even when an activity may place the client at risk. For example, a client with multiple sclerosis may have difficulty swallowing. To be safe, from a medical point of view, the client should not have any chunky hard food, because he or she could choke on it. If the client chokes, he or she could aspirate, which means that vomit can flow into the lungs. As a result, the client may get pneumonia, or he or she could die of suffocation from a piece of food lodged in his or her windpipe. Those are risks. Because the client knows the risks, he or she has the right to choose what he wants to eat.

Some nursing homes will ask a client to sign a waiver stating that the facility is not responsible for the client's choice of action, but it is debatable as to whether the waiver would stand up in court. To allow clients to make decisions about their health care, nurses need to protect themselves against repercussions of those decisions. Nurses will record on the client's chart what the client has been told about any adverse effects of a particular action. If the client is still determined to take the action, the nurse is absolved of responsibility through the charting procedure.

Appendix

RESOURCES

Armstrong, P., *Women, Privatization and Health Care Reforms: The Ontario Scan*, Working paper #10, National Network on Environments & Women's Health, York University, 1999.

BC Royal Commission on Health Care Costs, *Closer to Home Report*, Crown Publications Inc., Victoria, BC, 1991.

Burke, K.L. Todoruk, M. Pimental, C. & Rodych, C., "The impact of intra-institutional relocation on elderly residents living with dementia," Canadian Association on Gerontology Conference, Halifax, NS, 1998.

Canada Mortgage & Housing Corporation, "Housing Choices for Canadians with Disabilities," Ottawa, ON, 1992.

Canadian Institute for Health Information, *Canada's Health Bill*, Queen's Printer, Ottawa, ON, 1998.

Canadian Study on Health and Aging:

"Patterns for people with dementia in Canada," *Canadian Journal on Aging*, 13(4), 1996: 470–487.

Carlin, V.E., *Can Mom Live Alone? Practical Advice on Helping Aged Parents Stay in their Homes*, Lexington Books, Lexington, MA, 1992.

College of Nurses of Ontario, "Untie the elderly: A resource manual," *Communiqué*, September 2001:26.

Connidis, I., *Family Ties and Aging*, Butterworths, Toronto, ON, 1989.

England, Godkin & Onyskiw, *Outcomes of Physical Restraints Reduction Programs for Elderly Residents in Long-term Care: A Systematic Overview*, Alberta Professional Council of Licensed Practical Nurses, 1997.

Fletcher, P. & Hirdes, J.P., "Risk factors for serious falls among community-based seniors: Results from the national population health survey," *Canadian Journal on Aging*, 21(1), 2001.

Gambassi, G. Lapane, K.L. Sqadari, A. Landi, F. Mar, V. & Bernabei, R., "Measuring health outcomes of older people using the Sage database," *Canadian Journal on Aging*, 19(2) 2000: 67–86.

Gutman, G. & Blackie, N.K., *Aging in Place: Home Adaptations and Options for Remaining in Community*, Gerontology Research Center, Simon Fraser University, Vancouver, BC, 1986.

Hancock, T. & Perkins, "Mandala of health: A model of the human eco-system," *Family & Community Health*, 8(3), 1985: 1–10.

Hiatt, L.G., "The environment as a participant in health care," *Journal of Long-Term Care Administration*, 10(3): 1–17.

Hirdes, J.P., "A survival analysis of institutional relocation in a chronic care hospital," *Canadian Journal on Aging*, 15(4), 1996.

Kozak, J. Boustacha, E. Lukaweiki, J. McKean, E. & Wahl, J., "Enhancing Quality of Life in Long-Term Care Facilities," Round Table Discussion Canadian Association of Gerontology, Halifax, NS, 1998.

Kramer, J.S., "Who cares for the elderly? Formal and support," *Garland Studies on the Elderly in America*, Garland, New York, 1991.

Lawton, M.P., "The impact of environment on aging and behavior," In: Birren,

J.E. & Schaie, K.W. (eds.) *Handbook on the Psychology of Aging*, Van Norstrand Reinhold, New York, 1997: 276–331.

Marshall. V. (ed.), *Aging in Canada: Social Perspectives*, 2nd ed., Fitzhenry & Whiteside, Markham, ON, 1987.

McDaniel, S., *Canada's Aging Population*, Butterworths, Toronto, ON, 1986.

Ministry of Health & Ministry Responsible for Seniors, *Closer to Home Report*, BC Government, Victoria, BC, 1990.

Ministry of Health, National Research & Development Program, *Canadian Study on Health & Aging*, Queen's Printer, Ottawa, ON, 1998.

Ministry of Housing, Ontario, *Consultation Counts: Taking Action on a Housing Framework for Ontario*, Queen's Printer, Toronto, ON, 1992.

National Advisory Council on Aging, *The NACA* Position on Community Service in Health Care for Seniors, Ministry of Supply & Services, Ottawa, ON, 1990.

National Advisory Council on Aging, *Quality of Life in Long-Term Care Institutions; A Concerted Approach*, Ministry of Supply & Services, Ottawa, ON, 1992.

National Advisory Council on Aging, *Aging and the Health System: Am I in the Right Queue?*, Ministry of Public Works & Government Services, Ottawa, ON, 1998.

National Advisory Council on Aging, *1999 and Beyond: Challenges of an Aging Canadian Society*, Government of Canada, Ottawa, ON, 1999.

O'Rourke, N. Mclennan, R. Hadistauropoulos, T. Tuokko, H., "Longitudinal examination of the functional status of older adults: Successful aging within a representative Canadian sample," *Canadian Journal on Aging*, 19(4), 2000.

One Voice: The Canadian Senior's Network, *Habitat: A National Senior's Housing Consultation Final Report and Recommendation*, Ministry of the State for Seniors, Ottawa, ON, 1989.

Ontario College of Nurses, "Test your knowledge about consent," *Communiqué*, June 2002: 18–23.

PEI Association of Social Workers, *Learning Today for a Better Tomorrow*, Ministry of Health, Charlottetown, PEI, 1991.

Podnieks, E., *National Survey on Abuse of the Elderly in Canada: The Ryerson*

Study, Ryerson University, Toronto, ON, 1992.

Porter, S., Interview of Intake Coordinator, North Shore Region, Continuing Care Division, BC, 1999.

Regier, V. & Pynoos, J., *Housing the Aged: Design Directions and Policy Considerations*, University of California Press, Los Angeles, CA, 1987.

Sahyoun, N. Pratt, L. Lentzner, L. Dey, H. & Robinson, K., "The changing profile of nursing home residents 1985–1997," *Aging Trends* 4, March, Department of Health & Human Services, Center for Disease Control & Prevention, National Center for Health Statistics, Washington, DC, 2001.

Schulz, R. & Heckhausen, J., "A life span model of successful aging," *American Psychologist*, 51, 1996: 702–714.

Snow, J., Oral Presentation to Symposium on Long-Term Care, December 1–2, 1990.

Solace, P.D., "Aging is not inevitable decline," *Primary Care Geriatrics*, 4(3), 1996: 702–714.

Statistics Canada, *Population Projections for Canada, Provinces & Territories:*

1993–2016, (Catalog # 91-520) Ministry of Supply & Services, Ottawa, ON, 1994.

Teague, M.L. & McGhee, V.L., *Health Promotion: Achieving High Level Wellness in Later Years*, Brown & Benchmark, Iowa, 1992.

Telford, B. Pedlar, D. Salerno, J. Hohnke, N. & Schumann, J., *Total Care for the Aged — Models that Show the Way*, Symposium World Congress of Gerontology, Vancouver, BC, 2001.

The Ministries, *Partnerships in Long-Term Care: A New Way to Plan, Manage and Deliver Services & Community Support — Guidelines for Establishment of Multi-Service Agencies*, Queen's Printer, Toronto, ON, 1993.

Tognoli, J., "Residential environments," In: Stokols, D. & Altman, I. (eds.) *Handbook of Environmental Psychology*, 1, John Wiley & Sons, NY, 1987.

Wilson, J.W., "Assessing the walking environment of the elderly," *Plan Canada*, 21(4), 1982: 117–121.

World Health Organization, "Ottawa Charter for Health Promotion," *Health Promotion*, 19(4), 1986: III–V.